HOME OFFICE RESEARCH STUDY NO. 67

Crime Control and the Police:
a review of research

By Pauline Morris and Kevin Heal

A HOME OFFICE
RESEARCH UNIT
REPORT

LONDON: HER MAJESTY'S STATIONERY OFFICE

HOME OFFICE RESEARCH STUDIES

'Home Office Research Studies' comprise reports on research undertaken in the Home Office to assist in the exercise of its administrative functions, and for the information of the judicature, the services for which the Home Secretary has responsibility (direct or indirect) and the general public.

On the last pages of this report are listed titles already published in this series, and in the preceding series, *Studies in the Causes of Delinquency and the Treatment of Offenders.*

ISBN 0 11 340707 6

Foreword

The purpose of the present review is to draw together the findings of some of the more important and interesting pieces of research about the effectiveness of policing. Two conclusions warrant particular attention. First, the authors suggest that the police exercise a limited control over crime. Second, although the police may be less effective in controlling crime than traditionally supposed, they have a range of other important tasks to fulfil including the education of the public in how to avoid crime, the reduction of fear in the community, and the support of those who have recently become victims.

It is anticipated that the review, which forms part of a larger programme of work bearing on crime prevention, will be primarily of value to those concerned with the development of police research. It is hoped, however, that it will also serve as background to the developing debate regarding the role of the police during the 1980s and beyond.

Towards the close of 1979 Dr Pauline Morris, co-author of this review, died. It is appropriate, therefore, to record in this foreword the gratitude of her former colleagues for the contribution she undoubtedly made to criminology.

I J CROFT
Head of the Research Unit

January 1981

Contents

1 Introduction

The context chosen for this report is intentionally narrow, and the objectives limited. Its purpose is to review the literature pertaining to the effectiveness of the police in controlling crime, particularly the commoner forms of crime which make up the bulk of indictable offences such as burglary, assault, theft and the handling of stolen goods, car theft, shoplifting and criminal damage.

At the outset a distinction needs to be made between 'crime control' and 'law enforcement'. The law enforcement function of the police, the mandate for which stems from the penal code, is primarily concerned with bringing to justice those who have broken the law. 'Crime control', on the other hand, is considerably broader, and encompasses not only the enforcement of law but also a range of activities designed to encourage the citizen's respect for the law. Law enforcement then becomes one of a number of means of achieving crime control, not an end in itself: such means would include the maintenance of public order and the provision of social services. These broader means are addressed only insofar as they touch on the principal focus of the report.

In seeking to describe the myriad of duties assigned to the police, Bittner (1970, 1974) argues that the capacity of the police to *use coercive force* lends a unity to all police activity. If this explanation is accepted, and it is probably the best to hand, it might legitimately be argued that to deliberately divorce crime control from other aspects of police work for the purpose of this review, let alone to delimit the types of crime to be considered, is a questionable step. In practice, however, as Kelling (1978) noted, researchers have yet to test the hypotheses that police effectiveness in controlling crime is influenced by the way in which they undertake other aspects of their work. The need for research on such broad lines is undoubted. At the same time the present narrowly defined exercise can be justified partly because it helps to clear the ground for such research, but more particularly because it seeks to bring an understanding of some of the research that has been completed to the developing debate regarding police effectiveness in controlling crime. For many the correct and indeed only response to rising rates of crime is the allocation of additional resources to the police. In recent years this approach has attracted much political and public support. But during periods of economic hardship such a response may no longer be practicable even though public disorder and crime may well be expected to rise. Moreover, others, pointing to the very considerable resources already invested in the police and to the still rising rates of crime, challenge the traditional response and in doing so question what the

1

police actually do, and the extent to which their activities are related to crime control. It is to these questions that the present review is addressed.

Popular conceptions about the police are as much influenced by the mythology of the service as by the facts of its operation. This is hardly surprising since the mythology of policing is constantly presented and refurbished by the media, while relatively little is known about the practicalities of day-to-day police work. It is an obvious task, therefore, in the second and third chapters of this review to contrast the myths of policing (and the expectations derived from the myths) with information now available regarding routine police activities. In considering the effectiveness of these activities studies based on broadly similar sets of data have been grouped together. Thus, in Chapter 4 of the review, studies relying primarily on aggregate data (by this is meant data drawn from cross-sectional or longitudinal research designs) are considered, while the studies discussed in Chapters 5 and 6, which deal principally with police patrol and investigatory activity, rest on samples drawn from single areas at a particular time. At first sight aggregate studies, many of which examine the relationship between resources allocated to the police and subsequent crime rates, would seem the most appropriate way of assessing the impact of police activity on crime. However, given that such research must, of necessity, rest on gross measures not only of resources and police activity but also of the outcome of this activity, the interpretation of the findings is frequently difficult. In this review, therefore, more weight is attached to those studies appearing in later chapters which provide more precise information about police activities and the effectiveness of particular strategies in controlling crime. Many, if not all, of the studies considered during the course of this review lend weight to the conclusion that the traditional strategies adopted by the police have but a limited impact on crime; in view of this Chapter 7 considers the extent to which this apparent failure of the police can be attributed to the constraints, including economic constraints, under which the service operates. Chapter 8 examines alternative strategies that can usefully be developed in particular forms of 'community policing'. The review concludes with a brief discussion of future research.

Discussion of police effectiveness, even where set within the narrowest boundaries, inevitably raises the related but broader issue of police accountability. It has been recognised for some time that where improved performance stems from the use of certain specialist squads and tactics, accountability may stand in opposition to effectiveness. In practice, however, the notion of accountability impinges on *all* aspects of police work including community policing. This aspect of policing has attracted much attention in this country but little thought has been given to the implications of its development in terms of the accountability of the police to the community they serve. This important issue is raised in Chapter 9.

Two further points need to be made in this introduction. The first concerns the use of the term 'effectiveness' in the present review, a matter that will be discussed in more detail in Chapter 4. Since judgements about police effectiveness will vary according to the standpoint of the evaluator, and since various interest groups within society will hold differing views about effectiveness, any discussion of effectiveness must necessarily be relative. Furthermore, it should be recognised that factors outside the immediate control of the police play an important part in determining how effective the police can be. Thus, if the public are unwilling to report crime, or to tolerate police intervention in their lives, or if legislation is ambiguous making it difficult to bring offenders to trial, then such factors will inevitably place limits on police effectiveness.

The second point concerns the fact that the dearth of British research on police effectiveness has forced the authors of this report to rely very heavily upon North American work (cf. Clarke and Hough, 1980). Unfortunately there have been few cross-national studies, and it is therefore difficult to assess the extent to which North American empirical research and theorising is relevant to the British situation. Manning's book (1977) is based, in part, on British information, and he writes of the "Anglo-American police mandate". McCabe and Sutcliffe (1978) support this view noting there are "striking similarities between the practices of the police and the citizen in different countries and types of community... Revolutionary Paris, nineteenth century London and twentieth century Chicago seem to have had similar types of citizen misbehaviour to interpret and control".

Jefferson (1979), in his review of Manning's work, challenges this view noting that little has changed in the English mandate (Bunyard, 1978) whilst quite major transformations have occurred in the American one. To quote Jefferson: "The consequence is that Manning can, and does, use examples from either side of the Atlantic indiscriminately to make his point—and this despite the fact that he recognises the different social structures and histories of the two societies". Miller (1977a) also draws attention to the structural difference between the New York police and the London police in the period 1830–1870, and contrasts the distinctive styles of police authority and public image which have emerged as a result. Writing about the interplay between public morality and enforcement policy in a subsequent publication (1977b), he again refers to differences between the United States and Britain not only in respect of police behaviour, but also in the political dynamics whereby policy is created.

Nevertheless, while differences do exist between the American and British systems of policing, particularly, for example, with regard to the appointment of senior officers, the use of firearms and the pre-trial process, important similarities can also be found. Thus the limitations which impinge upon and constrain the performance of an officer of a North American force would no doubt be recognised by a British police officer; similarly while the amount of crime may vary from one country to the next the broad characteristics of crime are probably similar; for example, in both countries much crime is committed in private places and thus is inaccessible to the police, and that which is

3

committed in public is accomplished swiftly and without warning. It is also possible to point to similarities in the organisation of police work (particularly that undertaken by the lower ranks), in tactics, workload distribution and the nature of public demand. In the present report the view is taken that the similarities between the two police systems outweigh the differences, and that much can be learnt from study of the North American literature on police effectiveness.

2 The police role: myths and expectations

The importance of myths in society is referred to by Levi-Strauss (1966) who discusses the way people fit together "...the remains of events...odds and ends, to lead to a completed picture", and he refers to the untiring ordering and re-ordering of events and experiences in a constant search for meaning. Myths themselves are never true or untrue, real or unreal; they are a body of beliefs mediating and interpreting reality and they perform an important unifying function.

The mythology of policing leads both the police and many, if not all of their various publics, to hold certain shared expectations of their role in society. Popular conceptions about policing tend to draw on the metaphor of warfare: the police are engaged in a 'war against crime' (President's Commission on Law Enforcement and Administration of Justice, 1967). As a corollary of this the primary task for the police is seen by many as the suppression of crime and the pursuit of criminals; and the main weaponry in the war are strategies of deterrence. The preventive patrol, the detection of crime and the work of specialist squads are regarded therefore as tactics of central importance (Hough and Heal, 1979). The assumptions underlying this martial view of policing are open to question, nevertheless several factors (discussed below) work to sustain in the public mind the 'crime-fighting' image of the police. Of itself the popular image of policing would be of little interest, but as it undoubtedly plays some part in shaping the service offered to the public it warrants attention.

The mythology of policing finds support at a number of levels. First, the individual member of the public subscribes to the myth because he wishes to believe in the efficiency of the service and its ability in times of crisis or danger to place a policeman at his side within minutes. At the societal level, the situation is more complex since, by their very presence, the police symbolise the presence of the state in everyday life, and render explicit the state's interest in the maintenance of order. Insofar as the police are presented as people of integrity, they symbolise the congruence of moral values with those of the state, and those values inherent in the criminal law. Thus unless it is widely believed that the police are effective in ensuring that those who violate laws are punished, the laws themselves fall into disrepute and difficulties arise in the maintenance of social order. The idea is not new: Silver (1967) notes that from

5

their earliest days, the London police did not simply act as agents of legitimate coercion, but personified the view of those central institutions which brought them into being.[1]

Second, the police themselves emphasize the importance of their crime-fighting function at the expense of the more mundane aspects of police work. Reiner (1978) identifies six groups of officers within the service, each group having its own particular outlook on policy; however, almost all officers saw the social aspects of their work as "extraneous and on occasions counter-productive to proper police work". Walsh (1977) interviewed and observed a sample of London policemen, and found that the largest proportion of his sample were "action seekers", that is they regarded a "good cop" as one with the ability to solve crimes and make arrests. Crime control behaviour was highly valued by action seekers and emphasis was placed upon the detection rather than the prevention of crime.

A third way by which the crime fighting image of police work is sustained, and arguably the most important, is through the mass media. It is widely believed that people's perception of the police and their work is influenced by what they read in the papers, hear on radio and see on television. In supporting this view Sir Robert Mark (1971) argued, in his speech to the Institute of Journalists in November 1971, that the acceptability of the force depended upon its accountability—not least to public opinion which the mass media plays a significant part in forming.

There are a number of different ways in which the media influence public opinion. In the first place, the media tends to exaggerate the fear of crime (particularly serious crime) by virtue of the fact that it is the most heinous and lurid offences that receive greatest coverage (Cumberbatch and Beardsworth, 1976; Chibnall, 1977). The effects of the media on audience attitudes and beliefs about crime have not been researched in detail; commonsense suggests, however, that the stereotypical images of crimes, victims and offenders which are projected to the public must inevitably become imprinted upon people's minds, particularly if and when such views are reinforced editorially. Hall *et al.,* (1978) refer to a "signification spiral" by which is meant that the mere fact of reporting an event lends significance to it.

---

[1] Haller (1976) suggests that in the United States this has by no means always been the case; he notes that at the turn of the century, although the police in American cities were formally engaged in law enforcement, they were little orientated towards formal legal norms. Writing about Chicago in the nineteenth and early twentieth centuries, Haller notes not only the distance that separated police values from those of urban moralistic reformers, but equally how policies revealed much about the attitudes and forces that shaped police behaviour. In demonstrating the failure of the police to share the legal norms, Haller also observes that their behaviour mirrored what other groups in society expected of them including legislators and other arms of the criminal justice system; thus legislation was deliberately vague, and in ignoring legal rules they were simply reinforcing what others often defined as 'proper police behaviour'. He argues that only during the twentieth century have legal norms been brought to bear upon such behaviour, "at a gradually accelerating pace".

6

On the other hand, if one accepts the view that media reporting increases people's awareness and fear of crime, they will welcome, and tend to believe, any reassurance that the police are effectively controlling, preventing and deterring crime. In providing this reassurance the media are likely to be more influential than say the reports of academic research which point out that it is still a relatively rare event for any one individual to become the victim of an offence, particularly one committed by a stranger (Kelling, 1978). Chibnall (1977, 1979) argues that the media are a dominant institution in constructing images of policing for a mass audience, and draws attention to the importance the police attach to the process, referring in particular to Sir Robert Mark's press relations policy of improved access and information as a means of improving police/public relations. Arguably the issue is double-sided: not only do the police wish to reinforce public confidence in them, but at the same time the media are dependent upon the police who represent their main source of information regarding crime. Illustrating this point Chibnall argues that the scale of corruption within the Metropolitan Police may have been minimised by the media to maintain good relations with the police generally. Within this context Cox *et al.,* (1977) suggest that corruption was seen as a minority activity, explicable in terms of individual pathology rather than having its roots in certain features of police organisation.

Goldstein (1977) suggests that the training the police receive is to some extent based upon the myths about policing, and as a result does not provide instructions in how to deal with incidents the police most commonly handle. Perrier (1979), writing about the Canadian police, makes a similar point. Perrier also draws attention to the adverse effect that the perpetuation of the crime-fighting myth may have on attempts to increase police professionalism within the service.

Yet the more important consequence of the mythologies associated with the role of the police and the way in which they work lies elsewhere. As the number of recorded crimes increase (and victimisation studies such as those undertaken by Sparks *et al.,* (1977) and Hindelang (1976) estimate that only a very small percentage of crimes appear in police statistics) the police are faced with the dilemma of 'explaining', both to themselves and to the public, what might be regarded as their failure to control crime, whilst at the same time maintaining their crime-fighting image. At a practical, if somewhat superficial, level this is not too difficult, since the source of failure can be attributed by police and public alike to insufficient powers and lack of resources. American research has shown the general public do not blame the police for being ineffectual, rather they share the latter's belief that "more police, more stringent policing and less leniency by the courts" would resolve the problem (Biderman *et al.,* 1967). A survey by Harris and Associates (1972) showed that four out of five respondents believed that police and other law enforcement agencies should be tougher. Those in the 18—20 age group, non-whites and persons with incomes under $3,000 were least likely to support a tough

7

approach; but even among these respondents seven out of ten endorsed such a view. These results reflect a view that traditional modes of policing are essentially correct, and that the way to control crime is to allocate additional resources and/or powers to the police. While such views prevail, attempts to reappraise the role of the police in society and to develop alternative strategies for the prevention of crime will attract little support.

3 The reality of police work

The preceding pages have discussed the mythology of policing and suggested ways in which the crime fighting image is sustained. In discussing the reality of police work and the way policemen spend their time, this chapter first considers the tasks actually falling to the police, then, taking a different perspective, turns to the demand for police service arising from the public. Before proceeding, however, it is necessary to reiterate an earlier point, namely that each aspect of policing is inextricably bound to the next. The distinctions made in this chapter (e.g. between activities of the uniform branch and those of the criminal investigation department) are therefore to some extent artificial, being more easily found in the literature than in the practice of policing.

Setting aside the close interdependence between one aspect of policing and the next, there is ample evidence to suggest that much police time is spent on work not specifically related to crime. Martin and Wilson (1969), for example, in a study of twelve provincial forces and two divisions of the Metropolitan police, found that only 28% of total duty time was spent on crime matters in the provincial forces, 31% in the Metropolitan divisions. In practice these figures reflect, at least in part, the type of assistance the public seek of the police. Comrie and Kings (1975) on studying twelve areas of the country found that of all calls made to the police, 34% were concerned with criminal matters, 35% with incidents where some form of social service response was required, 17% with public order matters and 14% with traffic incidents. These findings broadly confirm the results of earlier work by Punch and Naylor (1973) who, on finding that some 59% of calls could be defined as "service requests", divided these into seven main groups: domestic occurrences; highway incidents; property (lost, found and abandoned etc.); people (missing and found etc.); errands; health; and animals. The more rural the area, the greater the probability that any call would be a request for service: 73% of calls in rural areas falling into this category as compared with 49% in urban. The authors claim that in making a "service request" the public wanted a "quick remedy from a reliable, authoritative but fatherly figure".

From Comrie and King's report, the broad conclusions of which are similar to those reached by Banton (1964), Cain (1971, 1973) and more recently by Hough (1980), it is possible to derive a breakdown of activities for the three main sections of the uniform branch: foot-patrol constables; area constables; and panda car drivers. This shows that only a small proportion of the time of uniform branch officers is concerned with crime. Details are shown in Table 1.

Table 1
On duty hours ('rounded' percentages) by activity & function
(Table derived from Comrie & Kings, 1975)

Activity	Foot patrol officer	Area constable	Panda driver
Car patrol	2	5	42
Foot patrol	53	47	8
Enquiries & visits	4	13	9
Crime incident	3	2	6
Traffic incident	2	2	3
Public order	2	2	3
Social service	2	2	4
Other*	31	28	22
	100	100	100

*This category includes the following activities: refreshments; report writing; traffic point work; off duty (for any reason), and non-visit beat work.

As might be expected, the task of dealing with crime falls primarily to officers attached to the criminal investigation department, who in this country comprise some 15% of all police officers.[1] Martin and Wilson (1969) report that members of the CID branches studied were responsible for some 56% of crime work occurring in provincial forces and 59% in the two metropolitan divisions. With the exception of beat officers, who undertook just under 25% of crime work, all other departments, including traffic, were involved in dealing with crime matters to only a very small extent. To provide a detailed picture of the work of CID officers the authors subdivide the time spent on duty according to function. The results are shown in Table 2.

Table 2
Allocation of active duty (as a %) by function—CID
(Derived from Martin and Wilson, 1969)

Type of force	Criminal investigation	Court work	Civil and other duties
Provincial forces	86	13	1
Metropolitan divisions	90	9	1
Special squads	95	5	—

From this table it is clear that something in the order of 10% of CID officers' time (possibly rather more in the provincial forces) is spent in court.

---

[1] This figure—derived from the records of Her Majesty's Inspectorate of Constabulary—obscures the fact that in some forces as much as 24% of police force strength is devoted to criminal investigation work, while in others—usually rural areas—as little as half these numbers are so engaged. It should be noted also that in many forces, particularly those of a predominantly rural nature, and to a lesser extent in the 'mixed' areas, some incidents, especially those of a less serious nature are investigated by uniform branch officers.

Since the study by Martin and Wilson was completed, a number of changes have taken place in the organisation of police force areas and to some extent in the organisation of the forces themselves. It is of interest, therefore, to find that the more recent study carried out by the organisation and development section of the Sussex police (1976) provides broad support for some of the more important findings to emerge from Martin and Wilson's research. The study shows, for example, that some 87% of the working day of the CID officers was devoted to duties in some way associated with crime and investigation. While only reflecting the activities of a single force, the study also provides valuable insight into the range of activities undertaken by CID officers. In practice, for example, it was found that only 28% of the officers' time was devoted solely to the task of investigation[2]; a further 22% falling under the heading of administration and the remainder of the time being distributed between the investigation of statements, taking statements, court work, briefings, discussions, interviews, patrol and observation work, supervision and a range of other duties, all of which the authors regard as being indirectly related to criminal investigation. When not engaged in criminal investigation work (13% of duty time) officers were engaged on escort duties, office manning or taking refreshment breaks.

The most detailed information regarding the time spent per crime is to be found in an unpublished report by Crust (1975). This shows that, taking the combined efforts of the uniformed and CID branch officers, on average 7.7 hours was spent per detected crime (this figure comprises 4.5 hours devoted to investigation and 3.2 hours to administration) and 3.5 hours per undetected crime (2.8 to investigations, 0.7 to administration). These figures are broadly similar to those appearing in the report by the Sussex Police when account is taken of the fact that Crust's figures do not include court and travel time. Not surprisingly, considerable variation is reported regarding the time spent on one crime in comparison with another. Thus, taking CID effort with regard to the investigation of detected crime, the study shows that on average 19.3 hours were devoted to offences of robbery, 8.2 hours to sexual offences and 6.4 hours to burglary in a dwelling. At the other end of the scale, crimes of going equipped to steal, shoplifting, criminal damage and other offences (Home Office Classification 62–99) attracted 1.5 hours or less of CID time. To be set against these figures are those for undetected crimes, and here the study shows that on average 7.7 hours were devoted to an undetected robbery, 14.9 to a sexual offence and 2.4 hours to a burglary.

The principal limitations of the studies discussed above arise from the fact that they rely heavily on records kept by the police themselves rather than upon independently collected data. Nevertheless, the main conclusions of the British studies, particularly those of uniformed officers, are confirmed by more

---

[2] For the purpose of the survey the term 'investigation' was defined as "all time spent interviewing the complainant, injured/aggrieved person, loser or witnesses, or seeking information from any service including police records, searching for marks or clues, questioning suspects".

methodologically sophisticated research carried out elsewhere. In the Netherlands, for example, a study of nearly 2,000 people who had called the police during a three year period found that 36% of calls were to request information and/or assistance, or were in connection with traffic incidents (Junger-Tas, 1978). American research presents a similar picture. Bercal (1970), for example, showed that in Detroit, New York and St Louis, amongst calls for assistance by a police *emergency* number, a significant number were dealt with without despatch of patrol — 36%, 40% and 21% of total calls respectively. Even when patrols were despatched, only approximately one-third of the incidents were defined by the police as related to crime. This study, together with other work by Wilson (1968), Westley (1970), Reiss (1971), and Kelling *et al.,* (1974) confirms that the popular image of the police as a crime fighting organisation is largely inaccurate. In practice, police work covers a range of activities only a proportion of which are directly related to the control of crime.

Before discussing studies more closely concerned with the crime control function of the police in the next chapter, it is important to acknowledge the part played by the public in shaping the demand for police service. Most studies indicate that about 70% of police work is in response to public demand Reiss, (1971). Yet there are certain dangers in regarding the police service as an organisation which merely responds to public demand. Implicit in this view is the unjustified assumption that there exists an undifferentiated public whose members act in similar ways when deciding whether or not to call the police. In practice, Ericson (1978), claims that the opinions and actions of some segments of the community are more influential than others, while Gelles (1976) goes so far as to suggest that the policeman is the poor man's social worker.

A second, and probably more important point, is that to see the police simply as responding to public demand ignores the element of negotiation which takes place between the police and the public. Chatterton (1976) and McCabe and Sutcliffe (1978) demonstrate clearly the way in which the police negotiate each encounter not according to any fixed rules or regulations, but in the light of their perception of cultural conditions and within their own organisational constraints. The policeman's concern with avoiding 'trouble', to which Chatterton also refers, must without doubt play an important part in determining how he responds to particular situations. Another factor is the stereotype that the police hold of individuals, both as suspects and complainants, and in this respect outward appearance may in some circumstances be more significant than the events or circumstances reported (McCabe and Sutcliffe, 1978).

Such findings have much in common with those reported in America by Skolnick (1966), who found that between 20% and 25% of burglary complaints were recorded as "suspected" offences and, as such, did not appear in the burglary statistics. He explained this in terms of the degree to which the complainant was able to justify himself or herself as the 'victim' or alternatively, whether the circumstances contained all the elements necessary to define them as a crime from the police perspective. While the data are not precisely comparable, information collected in this country by Sparks *et al.,* (1977) suggests that Skolnick's figure is on the low side. Sparks and his colleagues report that something in the order of two thirds of the crimes reported to the police by the public were not recorded in police statistics.[3]

---

[3] The findings of this study must be treated with caution, since the research was conducted in areas atypical of the remainder of the country.

4 Police effectiveness: a broad view

This chapter falls into two parts. In the opening section the concept of effectiveness is discussed and contrasted with the closely related but different measures of productivity and efficiency. The second part of the chapter is given to a brief discussion of 'aggregate studies' and the lessons that can be learnt from this approach to the study of police effectiveness.

A brief reference to the definition of 'effectiveness' appeared in the Introduction to this report, where it was noted that several factors served to constrain police effectiveness in controlling crime. The definition clearly requires some elaboration, particularly since, in some of the literature, the term appears to be used interchangeably with 'productivity' and even on occasion with 'efficiency'. Those seeking a fuller discussion of these terms than to be found in this review might turn to Hirsch and Riccio (1974) or to the more recent papers presented at a workshop on police productivity organised by the Solicitor General's Department, Federal Government of Canada (Engstad and Lioy, 1979).

Productivity is generally measured in terms of the amount of output obtained for a given input and it is widely defined as encompassing both effectiveness and efficiency (Hatry, 1975). Pollard (1979) suggests that the terms effectiveness and efficiency are frequently misused in relation to police work, with police officers attempting to prove their effectiveness by pointing to their efficiency in certain specific areas. He draws an analogy with a water pump working at maximum efficiency, i.e. giving maximum ratio 'output' to its 'input', but being completely ineffective in coping with water which is flooding at a greater rate than that which the pump is capable of handling. In applying this analogy to the police it can be seen that where objectives fall beyond their capacity, notions of police effectiveness have little or no meaning.

In general terms, effectiveness may be defined as the extent to which a particular resource is accomplishing its purpose, and for the most part it is assessed without regard to costs or other inputs, although an effectiveness *ratio* may be computed by dividing the amount of output achieved by the maximum potential output possible (Riccio, 1978). The clearance rate provides an obvious example since actual output can be divided by a measure of what output would be if the activity under consideration (i.e. police work) were 100% effective. Efficiency measures, on the other hand, indicate the degree to

14

which manhours, or other input resources designated to perform particular activities, in fact do so. In terms of patrol deployment, for example, an efficiency measure would be the ratio of manhours spent on the street to the total manhours worked by the officers assigned to such duties (thus indicating the amount of time 'lost' by roll calls, court appearances etc.).

The distinction between the terms is useful since an organisation may well be efficient but unless its activities accomplish the desired output it cannot be regarded as fully effective. Similarly, it may be deemed effective but if it is not running at minimal cost, or if its inputs are being wasted on conversion to output, it cannot be regarded as efficient. An organisation can only be regarded as achieving maximum productivity if it satisfies both considerations of efficiency and effectiveness, and although this review is primarily concerned with issues of *effectiveness*, of necessity the issue of efficiency also arises.

Nevertheless, even careful attempts to define the various terms both over-simplify the task and fail to take account of the unreliability of much of the basic data upon which subsequent measurement is predicated. The short-comings of criminal and police statistics are well known, yet they continue to form the basis of many researches. Equally, many definitions assume a value concensus regarding the objectives to be attained, whereas no such concensus exists. The point is made succinctly by Ball (1974):

> ...while the public vigorously affirms such notions as freedom, democracy and crime reduction in the abstract, individuals and interest groups often disagree violently with respect to who is to be granted what degree of freedom, as to how much democracy is to be tolerated under what conditions, and as to *what sorts of crimes should be reduced* and what methods are acceptable for the accomplishment of any such end.

Furthermore it is important to recognise that police *effectiveness* and *crime-control effectiveness* should not be confused. The importance of this distinction can be recognised by considering that one consequence of measurement in any organisation is for its members to concentrate on those activities that are capable of being measured—in the present case recorded crime, arrests, clearance rates, etc.—at the expense of those less tangible areas of activity which are difficult, if not impossible, to measure, such as crime prevention, social assistance and the maintenance of public order (Fisk, 1974). As a result, a situation could arise in which apparent increases in police effectiveness occurred without a commensurate increase in crime control. Unfortunately, warnings about definitions and other problems relating to the use of crime and police statistics have largely gone unheeded—or at best are acknowledged and then ignored—as is evidenced in some of the major studies of police effectiveness discussed in this review.

Studies of police effectiveness have been undertaken in a number of different ways and have examined a variety of questions, making comparison of results difficult. Not surprisingly no simple classification of the work is entirely satisfactory but it has been found useful to try and group together studies seeking to measure effectiveness on the basis of broadly similar sets of data. The following section of this chapter considers studies based on *aggregate* data, that is upon data gathered from a large number of police forces or jurisdictions, or alternatively from a single area but over a considerable number of years. Studies using such data vary considerably in their methodological sophistication and appear in the literature under a variety of headings: societal, macro, econometric, cross jurisdictional, longitudinal or aggregate studies. In the following discussion the term aggregate is used. In broad terms data are usually analysed with a view to comparing, between one area and the next or across time, manpower or expenditure levels and indices of police performance (arrest rates, clearance rates and/or crime rates). The approach stands in contrast to the more familiar method of analysing the impact of manpower or tactical change within an area by experimental or quasi-experimental methods. Studies based on these methods of evaluation are discussed in Chapters 5 and 6.

Aggregate studies

Aggregate studies have proceeded in a number of ways. Taking first those relating to arrest rates (the most popular measure of police performance) and levels of crime, Sjoquist (1973), Logan (1975), Phillips and Votey (1972), Tittle and Rowe (1974) all report lower levels of crime in areas where police arrest rates are high. In carrying out these studies most researchers have relied on official statistics, but in an attempt to overcome the known weakness of these figures a study by Wilson and Bolan (1976) examined data obtained from victimisation surveys. The authors compared arrest rates and the rates at which serious robberies were reported to interviewers in twenty six large American cities. Again, a strong negative correlation was found to persist.

Tittle and Rowe found that the negative association between arrest rates and reported crime was strongest where the probability of arrest was greater than 30%; where the probability of arrest was less than this, no association was found. This finding led the authors to suggest that there was a 'threshold' below which arrest was not effective. Brown (1978) provides further information on this point suggesting that a threshold effect was present in the smaller cities but not in the larger ones. Three possible explanations of these results exist: the threshold effect observed by Tittle and Rowe was spurious; the probability of arrest in large cities may not exceed the critical level necessary for the effect to operate; or public perceptions of the probability of arrest may be more accurate in smaller cities.

Where measures of resources (either in the form of policemen *per capita* or expenditure on police force *per capita*) are introduced to the analysis, a number of complications arise due to the inter-relationship of variables. For instance, the level of crime may influence the amount of police resources made available to deal with it but, simultaneously, police resources may have an impact on the level of crime. There is, therefore, some circularity that needs to be disentangled. Earlier studies, for example those by Allison (1972) and Pressman and Carol (1971) failed to address this problem. However, Carr-Hill and Stern (1979) developed three sets of equations to take account of the interactions probably existing between crime rate, clearance rate and police resources. The authors treated the equations as regression equations and estimated them simultaneously. The analysis, which was based on most police force areas in England and Wales and drew data from the census years 1961, 1966 and 1971, produced three principal findings:

  i. the higher the clearance rate the lower the crime rate;
 ii. the larger the number of police in an area the higher the recorded offence rate; and
iii. the larger the number of police in an area the lower the rate at which offences were cleared.

Carr-Hill and Stern attribute these results to the 'recording phenomena' whereby more police lead to more offences being recorded, either because the police discover more offences themselves or, more likely, because they record more of the offences reported to them by the public. While it would appear from the study that more police lead to lower clearance rates, Carr-Hill and Stern avoid suggesting that the police are ineffective, or do not have an effect in deterring criminals; rather they explain the finding by noting that the recording effect outweighs any deterrent effects, thereby causing the observed relationships. Similar results were obtained by Greenwood and Wadycki (1973) who again attributed the results to the effect of the recording phenomena.

To summarise the results of the more important of these studies, they have all found evidence of a strong inverse relationship between crime rates and clearance rates. Two studies (those by Carr-Hill and Stern and Greenwood and Wadycki) have found a positive relationship between crime rates and police resources. Only Carr-Hill and Stern measured the relationship between clearance rates and police resources which they found to be negative.

Difficulties arising in interpreting these findings and the various inconsistencies between the studies make it difficult to assess the value of the aggregate approach in studying the effectiveness of the police. While all the studies discussed find a strong inverse relationship between crime rate and clearance rate, it is quite unclear what implications are to be drawn from these results. On the one hand, such findings may be seen as providing evidence for the effectiveness of police activity; on the other, it can also legitimately be argued that the studies demonstrate a 'workload' effect, and that the clearance rates are high simply because crime rates of an area are low. Wilson and Bolan (1978) argued against this interpretation: using a cross-sectional sample of robbery, burglary and auto-crime in thirty five large American cities, the authors found no workload effect sufficiently large to challenge the deterrent hypothesis. Chaiken (1975) suggests, however, that in areas where workload levels are moderate, the association between this factor and arrests per crime is weak, while in areas where workload is either very low, or very high, its association with arrests is considerably stronger.

Setting these arguments aside (and it might be reasonable to assume that in certain areas under certain conditions the observed relationship between crime rates and clearance rates is not spurious) the positive relationship between crime rates and police resources remains to be explained. If police performance (measured by clearance rates) is associated with lower rates of crime, it is to be anticipated that increases in police resources would be accompanied by lower crime rates. However studies disagree on this point. It is of course possible that the findings of these studies are in fact an artifact of the statistics upon which they are based. This at least would explain the inconsistent pattern of results. The crime rate for example, as a measure of outcome of police activity, can be criticised on the grounds that it reflects only a small proportion of crime which actually takes place in a community (Sparks *et al.*, 1977) and, as many authors (McCabe and Sutcliffe, 1978; Coleman and Bottomley, 1976) have noted, the pattern of recorded crime is influenced by police discretion with regard to recording practices. Criticisms of the crime rate also apply to measurement of rates of clearance since the former is the denominator in the calculation for the clearance rate. In this country the pitfalls associated with using clearance rates as a measure of police activity have been discussed in much detail by Zander (1974), Coleman and Bottomley (1976) and Lambert (1970).

But the principal weakness of the aggregate approach to studying police effectiveness arises from the need to rely on gross data and the inability to draw from these data any indication as to how increased expenditure is to be most efficiently used or the way in which high clearance rates are achieved. A number of researchers have noted that the correlation between a number of officers allocated to a police department and the number appearing on street patrol is usually poor (e.g. Wilson, 1968). In subsequent publications (Wilson and Boland 1976, 1978) the authors also report that the crime rate may be less affected by the number of policemen on the streets than how they are deployed and what they do when they get there. Such a view is confirmed by Forst *et al.*, (1977) who showed that in Washington D.C. fewer than 10% of officers made over half the arrests, and nine accounted for more arrests than 450 of their colleagues.

To date the aggregate approach has yielded little useful information regarding the effectiveness of the police. If this method of study is to be of value the assumptions implicit in the approach require both modification and development. It will be necessary, for example, to take account of the factors influencing the reporting of crime, of the public's response to police activity, and of the way police manpower is deployed. Information of this nature can be gained from the type of studies discussed in the following chapters.

5 The effectiveness of patrol

In the view of O. W. Wilson (1963) the aim of the preventive patrol, a fundamental feature of police work, is to establish a sense of police visibility, to create a feeling of police 'omnipresence' and thereby to reduce crime. While intuitively a reasonable expectation, it is only recently that the effectiveness of patrolling in the prevention of crime has been empirically examined.

i. General patrolling
In one of the earliest studies to assess the effectiveness of the motorised patrol, Press (1971) showed that following a 40% increase in patrol manpower in the 20th precinct of New York City, reported crimes visible from the street decreased significantly in comparison with two nearby precincts.[1] However, apart from larceny and burglary, the number of crimes committed in places out of sight of patrol officers did not decrease significantly; a displacement effect was also observed, although the increase in crime in the adjacent area was found to be smaller than the decrease in the 20th precinct.

In commenting on Press's work, J. Q. Wilson (1975) notes that these apparently impressive results are inconclusive since only changes in reported crimes were observed and not changes in the number of crimes actually committed. Moreover, Wilson continues, the reporting system itself changed early in the project, a development that may well have affected the findings. A more serious difficulty stems from the fact that the reported decreases in crime were decreases *relative to expected levels of crime* and that in absolute terms the crime rates remained fairly stable in the experimental precinct.

Fisk (1970) found no evidence that increases in the number of cars patrolling an area led to crime reduction, a result confirmed by the more sophisticated work of Kelling *et al.,* (1974). In the well known Kansas City preventive patrol experiment Kelling examined the effects of varying patrol strength. In five "reactive" beats, vehicles entered only in response to calls for service; in five control beats, the "normal" patrol level of one car per beat was continued, while in five "proactive" beats, two or three marked cars patrolled each beat area. Findings of the experiment indicated that there were no significant differences among the areas in reported crime, rates of victimisation or level of citizen satisfaction with the police.

---

[1] While it is unclear from the original report whether the increase in manpower was allocated to foot or car patrol an unpublished paper by Kelling (1977) specified that the evaluation was undertaken with respect to motorised patrol.

Critics of the study (Larson, 1976; Fienberg *et al.,* 1976) claim that in practice visible police presence (whether achieved by random patrolling or through responding to calls) did not vary substantially between the three areas, and that even in the 'proactive' area the level of patrolling achieved did not adequately reflect routine levels of patrolling existing in other American cities. These criticisms cannot be entirely dismissed. Nevertheless, the Kansas City study lends weight to the conclusion that relatively *small* absolute increases in patrol manpower are unlikely to have a noticeable effect on reported criminal activity. Wilson (1975) supports this view; setting aside the methodological difficulties of Press's study, however, he draws on the research to suggest that *substantial* manpower increases are likely to reduce street crimes at least for a short period of time, though this may only be true for highly visible crimes such as street robbery.

But the results of a carefully monitored study by Schnelle *et al.,* (1977) indicate that Wilson's conclusion itself may require qualification. Schnelle and his colleagues observed that while a substantial increase in night patrol activity was accompanied by a decrease in crime, a similar decrease did not occur when day patrolling was increased. The authors explain this finding by noting that at night more crime occurs in city and town centres, and that these centres are easier to patrol than residential areas—particularly at night when traffic and pedestrians are few. Since the level of crime rose immediately additional patrol strength was withdrawn, Schnelle questions whether intensive patrolling can be justified—even at night—on cost/benefit grounds.

It is a central tenet of policing that the probability of making an arrest is increased by swift responses to calls for assistance. Much effort and techno-logical ingenuity has been devoted, both in this country and elsewhere, to reducing response time in the expectation that the number of arrests made would be increased, that the deterrent value of patrol enhanced, and that the public would be more satisfied with the service received. That these ends are achieved finds limited support in the evaluative studies undertaken by Isaacs in Los Angeles (1967) and Clawson and Chang in Seattle (1977). However, the results of a major study by Bieck (1977) show that the outcome of a large proportion of more serious crimes is not influenced by the speed of response, and that on those occasions where a fast response is necessary, the time taken by members of the public to report the incident is crucial.

Bieck divided total response time into three components: the time taken to report an incident, to despatch police resources and to travel to the scene of the incident. He studied only 'Part I' crimes (those of a more serious nature) dividing these into two groups: those discovered after the crime had occurred and the suspect left the scene (62%), and those in which a member of the public, either as a victim or witness saw, heard, or became involved at any point during the commission of the offence (38%). For the first category, described as "discovery" crimes, it was found — for obvious reasons — that the chances of making an arrest at the scene of the crime or locating a witness was not enhanced by rapid response. For the second category — "involvement" crime — the importance of response time was found to vary with the nature of the incident. However, since for all crimes studied, reporting time amounted to nearly one half of total response time, the time taken by the public to report a crime was the primary determinant of the eventual outcome. Thus, where an involvement crime was reported within one minute, the chances of making an on-the-scene arrest were 10 – 15% higher than in those cases where the public took five minutes to call the police. For burglaries the figure rose to 40%. Where the public took longer than five minutes to call the police — and this was found to be so for half of the involvement crimes studied — reporting time was no longer associated with the chances of making an arrest. In summary, therefore, Bieck's study — which has the advantage of being based on more reliable data than earlier work discussed — leads to the conclusion that only a small proportion of even the more serious crimes warrant rapid police response.

On examining why delay occurred in calling the police, Bieck found that on many occasions the public, being unsure as to whether police intervention was necessary sought the advice of others (friends, relatives or superiors at work), or simply waited and observed the scene of the incident in the hope of gaining additional information. Public satisfaction with the service received was found to be unrelated to the actual time taken to respond — the important factor was whether response time was perceived to be faster or slower than that expected, 87% of the public being satisfied with response time. An earlier study by Pate *et al.,* (1976) reached similar conclusions.

It has frequently been observed that the principal disadvantages of patrolling an area by car arises from the isolation of the police from the public and the area for which they are responsible. Under these circumstances contact with more than a handful of people is difficult, thus prejudicing police/community relations; it is also difficult for patrol officers to get to know their area or to establish more than a few sources of information. Many have noted that, freed from these disadvantages the officer patrolling on foot is likely to carry out the task of policing more effectively, particularly in busy congested city centres (Kelling, 1977; President's Commission on Law Enforcement and the Administration of Justice, 1967).

One of the first studies to evaluate the effectiveness of foot patrol was carried out in September 1954 by the New York City Police Department. During the study the police strength assigned to the 25th precinct in Manhattan (comprising much of East Harlem) was more than doubled. The strategy was apparently successful since during the four months of the experiment serious crimes declined, the reduction being greatest for crimes occurring in public places. Unfortunately the study, the results of which were used to attract further resources for the department, not only suffered from serious methodological weaknesses (Wilson, 1975) but was the subject of "data rigging" by the police (Farmer, 1980).

Similar problems beset the New York City Subway Project carried out between 1965 and 1973. At the beginning of the project the number of officers deployed in the New York subway system was increased from 1,200 to 3,100, the additional staff patrolling every station and train between eight p.m. to four a.m. Findings again indicated that the number of reported felonies and misdemeanours decreased immediately after the manning change and remained approximately constant for two years. Only after the study was completed and preliminary conclusions drawn did it become known that patrol officers had been encouraged to record crimes that occurred between 8 p.m. and 4 a.m. as having occurred at other times. Nevertheless, Chaiken (1974) in reinterpreting the findings in the light of this disclosure reached the conclusion that the increase in manpower probably did result in some reduction of crime; the only consequence of the data manipulation being to distort the magnitude of the effect.

A rather more complex study was carried out in four British cities by Bright (1969). During this experiment, which lasted for one year, the number of officers walking designated foot beats was systematically varied from zero to four. At the end of the year the study suggested that the number of reported crimes per beat decreased when the number patrolling rose from zero to one, but no further decrease was reported when patrol strength was increased to two per beat. There was some rather weak evidence that further increases in manpower would produce further reductions in crime. Unfortunately as the beats in which the experiment was conducted were small, and the period during which the changes made were brief, the results of the experiment can at best be regarded as tentative.

Schnelle *et al.,* (1975), in a study of the introduction of beat officers (walking patrols) to areas of Nashville, Tennessee, found that while the increases in patrol manpower were accompanied by an increase in the level of crime reported by the public, there was no change in the number of arrests. Heller (1977) reported very little measurable effect of allocating additional officers to foot patrol duties in an area of St. Louis.

A study recently completed in New Jersey assessed the impact of foot patrol activity on both crime and the public's perception of crime and public behaviour (Kelling and Pate, 1980). The study has shown that there appears to be little or no relationship between the level of crime occurring in a particular area and the number of officers patrolling there. It was found, however, that residents noticed changes in the number of officers patrolling the area in which they lived, and in those areas where the number of patrol officers was increased residents saw the severity of crime decreasing. This was not so for commercial respondents (shop-keepers, businessmen etc.). It was also found that residents in areas of increased foot patrol activity were more likely to forego protective measures against crime than residents in areas where the level of patrolling remained unchanged or had ceased. The authors conclude by noting that while foot patrol does not have a significant effect on crime levels,

22

it does influence residents' fear of crime and the protective measures they take to avoid crime.

The most optimistic conclusion to be drawn regarding the effectiveness of patrolling on foot or by car, is that very substantial increases in patrol manpower, or alternatively the introduction of patrol to an area where none had previously existed may, on occasions, lead to a reduction in particular types of crime though for only short periods of time. It can of course be argued that until some of the more important studies have been replicated, it is difficult to judge how great the increase in manpower must be before an effect on crime patterns is likely to be observed. There is some weight to this argument and it is likely that during the next two to three years work of this nature will proceed. However, the more interesting and probably more useful line of enquiry would be to seek out the reasons accounting for the 'failure' of the traditional patrol.

Some explanations are already to hand. Larson (1972), for example, has commented on the mis-match between police patrol effort and calls for service. Drawing on a study carried out in New York City in 1969, he notes that 54% of the day's calls for service were received during a period (four a.m. to midnight) when only 23% of the day's total patrol effort was made. Elliott (1973) puts forward an alternative explanation arguing:

> ...that the patrol's effectiveness against crime is limited because of its non-crime service function...the time the patrol does have to devote to anti-crime activities is available only in short time segments...(thus the patrol officer)...cannot plan his autocrime patrol since he has no way of predicting how much time he will have or when the time will be available.

Elliott dismisses the argument that the non-crime activities performed by the patrol aids crime control as "pure, unadulterated sophistry".

The obstacles to the development of effective policing identified by Larson and Elliott, can, and to some extent have, been overcome. Some forces, both in this country and elsewhere, have devised complex duty rotas enabling increased patrol effort during those periods when calls for assistance are high, or by dividing total patrol strength into crime and non-crime divisions. However, while such tactics are likely to lead to some improvement in effectiveness, the major factor impeding police performance stems from the nature of crime itself. A number of authors have made the obvious, if often forgotten and useful point, that a patrol can only prevent or intercept those crimes occurring in places accessible to the patrol officer. While *some* crimes do most frequently take place in public places — for example robbery (Nicholls and Bannon, 1972) — it has been estimated that something in the order of 40% to 45% of all crimes are committed in public places, leaving some 55% to 60% of crime beyond the reach of even the most efficient patrol (Elliott, 1973). Moreover, the crime which occurs in public is often accomplished quickly, stealthily and without warning. Thus the chances of the police witnessing or

23

being in a position to intervene even in these crimes are small. A second difficulty arises from the fact that while the aggregated crime statistics seem to represent an overwhelming problem, the number of incidents is *relatively* small if account is taken of the large number of opportunities for crime to be found in the activities of the population of even a moderately sized city during the course of a single day. Studies have shown that the likelihood of a uniformed patrol officer intercepting a crime in progress is very small; for example, a report of the president's Crime Commission estimates that a patrol officer in a large American city could expect to intercept a street robbery in progress once every fourteen years (President's Commission, 1967). While in this country Mayhew *et al.,* (1979) have noted that *on average* a household will be burgled once every 35 years — assuming that is, that around twice as many burglaries occur as are reported to the police.

ii. Specialised patrol

There is some evidence to suggest that changes in the organisation and structure of patrols, as distinct from simply increasing manpower, may improve crime control. In broad terms, alternative forms of patrol — variously called aggressive patrol, crime attack patrol, specialised patrol, high impact anti-crime programmes, (Kelling, *et al.,* 1980) — involve the assignment of officers to specific locations for the explicit purpose of controlling particular crimes. Such forms of patrol might involve the use of disguises, the use of unmarked vehicles, surveillance tactics or alternatively the creation of a highly visible patrol presence. Wilson and Boland (1976, 1978) distinguish between two extreme strategies of policing: "aggressive" and "passive". The former maximises police intervention in and observation of the community, the latter discourages the questioning of suspicious persons and does permit the use of 'decoy' or 'stakeout' procedures in areas of high crime rates.[2] The importance of this distinction in police practice is supported by research findings in San Diego (Boydstun, 1975) which showed that one component of aggressive patrol strategy (field interrogations or street stops) was signficantly associated with a decline in certain kinds of crime. In the experimental area (i.e. where field interrogations were stopped) crimes such as robbery, burglary, theft, autotheft, and assault rose by about a third, whereas there was no change in the frequency of such crimes in the control areas where field interrogation practices remained unchanged. However, bearing in mind earlier comments concerning the potentially unsatisfactory nature of arrest rates as a measure of police effectiveness, it is worth noting that the presence or absence of field interrogations did not affect the number of arrests in either area.

Pate *et al.,* (1976) evaluated a more ambitious project employing three criminal apprehension strategies: Criminal Information Centre (CIC) estab-

---

[2] The legitimacy of aggressive preventive patrol strategies has been questioned on the grounds that they alienate citizens and in particular minority groups; the President's Commission on Law Enforcement and the Administration of Justice, Task Force Report: *The Police* (1967).

24

lished as a clearing-house for information regarding target criminals which was distributed throughout the police department; Location Orientated Patrol (LOP) to carry out surveillance work in high crime areas; and a Perpetration Orientated Patrol (POP) to observe and record the activities of selected criminals.

Due to the difficulty of maintaining administrative control over the experiment the conclusions drawn are rather tentative. However, the study appears to have demonstrated that target criminals, about whom information was circulated by the CIC, were arrested more frequently than a group of comparable criminals, albeit, for minor offences. However, this result was achieved by conventional patrols not by the LOP or POP squads. It was also shown that the LOP squad was more successful in obtaining sound arrests than the POP group, but at the expense of increased complaints against the police.

In practice, specialised patrol is frequently comprised of a number of different activities. The New York City street crime unit, for example, adopted surveillance tactics, stop and search procedures, and the use of decoys in the bid to reduce street crime. Hapler and Ku (1975) note that the efforts of the street crime unit appeared to reduce levels of crime in certain precincts athough these effects could not be attributed with absolute certainty to the unit's activity. The most tangible outcome of the unit's work was to be found in the fact that the arrests made by members of the unit resulted in an impressively high rate of convictions, while at the same time injuries to the public, the police, and the perpetrators of the crime, were kept to a relatively low level.

A similar but smaller project, mounted in a bid to reduce street robbery, is described in a paper by Nichols and Bannon (1972). In this particular study, a crime analysis showed that of some 23,000 robberies conducted in Detroit in 1970 nearly 18,000 occurred in the streets in full view of the public. To combat this a 'zero visibility patrol' was mounted in which police officers patrolled in two's or three's usually in plain clothes and accompanied by mobile patrols in unmarked cars. As a part of the strategy officers would wear disguises and act as decoys. While the project was not evaluated with the same care as the New York experiment, anecdotal evidence suggests that the use of decoy tactics again resulted in an increase in the number of arrests leading to convictions. In the first eight months of the operation, however, eight offenders were killed by police officers and 38 police officers were wounded, one fatally. While the subject of much press criticism, the authors report that many members of the community, particularly black members who had experienced street crimes in the past, supported this aggressive form of patrolling.

One of the most valuable studies carried out on patrol specialisation is that by Tien et al., (1978). This evaluated an experiment to test the efficacy of the split-force patrol concept based on a separation of the call for service response and the crime prevention functions of a police patrol. To achieve this method of policing it was necessary to increase the efficiency of the call for service response (the basic patrol) so that a dedicated preventive patrol (the structured patrol) could be formed. This was done by ensuring that the basic patrol units were deployed in better proportion to the temporal distribution of calls from the public for assistance and by giving each call for service a priority. The dispatch of cars could, if necessary, be officially delayed in non-critical cases (86% of all calls). Furthermore, since many of the calls were routine, the number of patrol units manned by two officers was reduced. The structured patrol had the primary function of preventing crime, being directed in its activities by a special operations unit which provided crime analysis information. It was also expected however to provide a back-up service for the basic patrol in felony incidents, and if necessary to respond to urgent calls for service. As a result of the experiment, which lasted for one year with a six month test period, the level of Part I crime (the more serious offences) decreased slightly (6.1%), and Wilmington residents remained satisfied with the service received. Moreover, as a result of the conversion to single officer cars, the efficiency of the basic patrol unit in terms of calls for service per patrol officer increased by over 20% without apparently jeopardising the safety of the officers. The structured patrol units contributed to a substantial (105%) increase in the clearance of Part I crimes by the patrol division at the expense of the detective division whose own clearance fell by 61%. Overall there was an 18% increase in manpower efficiency. The success of the patrol division in clearing crime was primarily attributed to the *immediate* investigation of felony carried out by officers of the structured patrol, who, given the paucity of preventive tactics, were willing to undertake investigative work. The authors of the report conclude by referring to the fact that little attention has been given to developing patrol methods for affecting crime prevention (most patrolling tactics being directed to apprehension); they note also that the experiment led to a lack of communication and co-operation between the units but suggest that this could be mitigated by more careful organisation of the units' work.

Elliott (1973), to whose work reference has already been made, argues in effect that the performance of the traditional vehicle patrol can be improved. Assuming that a mobile patrol could be organised in a way that would allow "significant blocks of time" (between three to four hours) to be devoted to anti-crime work, Elliott examines how the patrol can be deployed over time and place so as to maximize its probability of preventing and intercepting crime, and of making immediate apprehensions. Elliott concludes that an officer who patrols in a "random manner"[3], and drives at a predetermined speed, will be more effective in controlling crime than his colleague who patrols at his own speed a route selected in a non-random way. This method of

---

[3] By "random manner" Elliott means that there is no fixed or quasi fixed sequence by which the patrol visits each target point in an area yet all are visited within the same average time.

patrolling (which Elliott calls interception patrolling) formed a part of the strategy adopted by the crime control teams introduced to the Syracuse New York police department in 1968. Elliott concludes that use of a computer designed patrol route would increase interception probability by some 50% over a route selected by the most experienced patrol officer.

Elliott challenges traditional views about the operation of the mobile patrol in two ways. First, he notes that many officers reduce their probability of intercepting a crime by driving *very* slowly in order to see everything. Elliott maintains that this is ineffective, and that the probability of detecting crimes occurring in the patrol area can be increased by driving at a speed of between seven to ten miles per hour. Second, in considering the operational advantage of two-manned patrol car versus those manned by one officer, Elliott concludes that the interception rate of one-man patrols is superior.

In bringing operational research methods to police deployment strategies Elliott and his colleagues provide some explanation of the poor performance achieved by traditional patrolling methods and offer one view of the way in which patrolling might be improved. Yet in reviewing Elliott's work it is important to note that some of the assumptions upon which it rests are probably unrealistic,[4] and the estimates of important probabilities, and time factors possibly imprecise. More importantly given the poor performance of traditional patrols it is unlikely, even in the event of the intercept strategy leading to a 100% improvement in effectiveness, that the net result would justify the costs of withdrawing the patrols from non-crime activities.

A police tactic designed to complement specialised patrol work in dealing with property crime is the anti-fencing operation. This approach to the control of crime is designed to assist the police through undercover operations in apprehending both thieves and 'fences', to recover stolen property and more importantly to disrupt stolen property markets. A report prepared for the LEAA by the Westinghouse National Issues Centre (1979) reviews 20 anti-fencing (Sting) operations and studies three in some detail. At the time of writing none of the projects had been completed, but the authors conclude that data to hand present a positive "if cloudy picture of the impact of the projects on the property crime rate". In practice while all three projects studied showed some decreases in property crime, in only one case was the decrease statistically significant. However, of the arrests made during the operations an unusually large proportion resulted in conviction.

There is some evidence to suggest therefore that specialised police tactics may have an effect on crime. On the one hand tangible improvements in the status

---

4 Important assumptions underlying Elliott's work are: (i) that significant percentage of crimes can (a) be prevented by police presence; (b) intercepted by the police; and (c) brought to the attention of the police soon enough so that there is a possibility of making an immediate apprehension; (ii) that there is a definite time interval during which the prevention, interception or immediate apprehension tactics can be exercised effectively.

of a particular task, appears to lead to an improvement in police performance, though this may prove to be only a short term gain. On the other hand and of greater importance, are the gains which appear to be achieved as a result of differentiating between police tasks, and of developing specific police tactics. However, as the studies discussed have demonstrated, such a strategy may incur costs in the form of public alienation from the police, or rivalry between one group of officers and the next.

6 Criminal investigation

The second and most prestigious arm of police activity is that concerned with criminal investigation. By popular conception the detective holds particular, possibly unique, professional skills which justify the elite position he holds within the police service. Drawing on the work of Skolnick (1966) and of Werthman and Piliavin (1967), Matza (1969) lends some support to the popular view of the detective. He distinguishes between the classical mode of suspicion — in which the offence itself, and those who had an opportunity or motive to commit it — provide the focus for the investigation, and the bureaucratic mode, where the main investigative tactic is to search for a suspect amongst those previously known to the police for having committed similar offences. In Matza's view the investigation of most criminal offences follows the bureaucratic mode. However this view is challenged in a paper by Reiss and Bordua (1967) who observe that the majority of cases cleared by arrest solve themselves in the sense that the offender is known to the police or the complainant at the time the crime is reported. In a later paper (1971) Reiss confirms this earlier impression noting:

> There is a paradoxical relationship between the way in which detective work is organised to solve crimes and how crimes are actually solved. Police departments ideally organise detective divisions to solve those crimes that require intensive investigation. Yet we maintain that most of the knowledge that contributes to the solution through investigation is based on citizen information on the identity of the suspect.

Since Reiss's work, a number of major American studies on criminal investigation have continued to challenge the popular conception of detective activity by suggesting that for the most part detectives work on crimes that are easily cleared rather than upon difficult cases (Greenwood et al., 1977; Bloch and Bell, 1976; Elliott, 1978). Greenwood et al., note that differences in the training, staffing, workload and procedures of detective departments appear to have no appreciable affect on crime, arrest or clearance rates, and that the organisational structure of the force appears unrelated to such rates. The one exception concerns "difficult target offences" (i.e. serious crimes) where investigating officers are seen to have a potential ability to increase arrest rates, provided they deal only with crimes of this nature.

A study by Sanders (1977) differs in its perspective from those by Greenwood and Bloch and Bell in that it is concerned with the way information determines much detective work. The research examines the information, resources, and

29

strategies of three organisational units — juvenile, burglary and major crime — which together dealt with a wide spectrum of cases. According to Sanders, the decision to investigate an allegation is not based on the nature of the crime that has been committed, nor upon the need to establish a good clearance rate, but on an interpretation of the facts reported as to whether or not the case constitutes a 'real' crime. There are, he argues, shared departmental assumptions regarding the nature of crime and criminals, a situation that may account for the low status afforded to the juvenile unit which dealt with a wide variety of 'petty' offences. In the case of the burglary unit, the fact that they are faced with a regular stream of cases offering few leads results in most cases being immediately "inactivated". On the other hand, the major crime unit which dealt with a variety of serious cases is afforded high status, and the task of investigation is generally said to be easier, most cases having an eye-witness if not a suspect from the outset. However, the high conviction rate achieved by this unit had little apparent impact on the level of crime in the area.

Most studies of criminal investigation have given much attention to the amount of time devoted to detecting crime. Greenwood *et al.,* for example, have observed that detectives "spend some 40% of their time in an interruptible fashion on other activities" (i.e. not involved in crime solving). In regard to the regional police force in Canada, Ericson (1978) notes that something in the order of a third of detective time was related to specific cases or suspect investigations; as much as half their time was found to be spent in the office typing reports, reviewing files, at formal and informal meetings and on office routine work — a figure not dissimilar from that reported by Greenwood *et al.*

Until recently, comparatively little work had been undertaken to study British detectives and the effectiveness of their methods. A partial picture could be drawn from a number of studies which, for the most part, have been primarily concerned with issues other than the investigation of crime (e.g. Bottomley and Coleman, 1976; Woodley, 1976). It is therefore of interest to consider three recently completed studies, the first by Steer (1980), the second by Mawby (1979) and the third by Bottomley and Coleman (1980).

Steer reports findings similar to those of earlier American work. Thus with regard to the skills of detectives he reports that in the majority of cases the detection of crime involves little of what the public would perceive as real detective ability:

> The success of the police in the detection of crime depends for the most part on how much useful information the public is able to give the police about the circumstances of the events. It is difficult to see how the situation could be otherwise.

In discussing the investigation of cases, Steer notes that it is the primary task for the investigating officer to look immediately for some indication of the suspect's identity. If an identification offering a reasonable chance of success is found, the case is pursued in the hope of clearing it. If, however, there is no immediate indication of identity the case is unlikely to be pursued much further. In qualifying this broad characterisation Steer notes that offences perceived as more serious attract more investigatory effort whatever the initial hope of success might be.

Around 57% of offenders responsible for incidents studied by Steer were caught as a result of being at or near the scene of a crime, or actually committing a crime when the police arrived, or because the police were given their identity by the victim or witness. For this group, Steer suggests the detections could have been made by the average man in the street were he given the appropriate legal knowledge. Of the remaining 43% of offenders, approximately 12% were detected as a result of being stopped and checked by police, on the basis of information received from the public, as a result of local police knowledge, or from a fingerprint search. Between 12% and 13% of offenders were identified as a result of being implicated during the course of a police interrogation. The remaining 18% were detected because they had the opportunity to commit the crime being investigated, were in possession of stolen property, caught while disposing of stolen property, or as a result of police observation or a police trap. On reviewing these and other findings Steer concludes that the business of detecting offenders was relatively straightforward in all but 25% of the cases studied.

For Steer one of the principal investigatory skills of the police lies in knowing how to act upon information the public provide. He also points, however, to the skill of the police in interviewing suspects. In supporting this view Steer notes that a large proportion of offences studied were cleared as a result of interviewing the suspects at a police station following arrest for some *other* offence, or as a result of stolen property being found in the suspect's possession. Offences detected in this way comprise some 41% of detections in a random sample of all indictable offences occurring during the study period, and 20% of a sample of more serious offences.

The study by Mawby (1979) largely confirms the figures presented by Steer. On examining the way in which a sample of standard list offences committed in nine areas of Sheffield were detected, Mawby found that just under 40% were detected "indirectly", that is as a result of routine police interviews with offenders caught for *other* offences. Of offences detected "directly", 62% were solved as a result of information given by the public which led the police directly to the offender, leaving some 38% of "direct" detections— some 23% of all detections — attributable to police investigatory effort.

Further evidence regarding the importance of the police interviews in detecting crime is to be found in a study of police interrogation by Softley *et al.,* (1980). On the basis of a study conducted in four police stations, Softley reports that nearly half of the suspects who were interviewed made a confession, and over two thirds gave information which would help secure a conviction. However, in considering the consequences of curtailing police powers to question suspects, Softley qualifies his findings regarding the importance of interviewing. He notes that in only 8% of cases studied did the police officers interviewed admit that it would have been necessary to drop the case if the suspect had refused to answer questions.

Further insight into crime investigation work, and to some extent further qualification of some of the more interesting conclusions reported by Steer, is to be found in a paper by Bottomley and Coleman (1980). The authors, whose paper is principally concerned with the limitations of official crime rates as a measure of police effectiveness, note that in 26% of detected cases studied the police were presented with a ready-made solution at the scene of the crime, and thus 'real' detective work was unnecessary. For a further 26% of cases, detection occurred as a result of questioning by the police, while 24% were detected by means of information from complainants, victims or witnesses. The number of cases detected as a result of activities more closely akin to public stereotypes of real detective work (e.g. on the basis of information received from informants, contacts — formal or informal — or intelligence systems), accounted for 5% of detections. Special police enquiries, such as finger printing, forensic tests, house to house enquiries, accounted for 2%, while 'set ups' or 'plants' accounted for a further 2%. Three percent were cleared up as a result of police vigilance (i.e. powers of observation and quick-wittedness of police officers). The remaining cases, where information was available, were accounted for either by the offender giving himself up or by admitting to the offence while in prison. The authors are, however, more sceptical than Steer of the investigatory skills of CID officers, and point to the fact that in those cases where suspects were identified by the police, much of the work was undertaken by officers from the uniform branch; an observation which clearly implies that in practice it is quite incorrect to see the 'expertise' for investigation residing solely in the hands of officers allocated to criminal investigation departments (cf. Chatterton, 1976). On a second point, when considering the importance of questioning procedures in terms of identifying suspects, Bottomley and Coleman note all but twelve of the 270 cases detected as a result of questioning were in practice cleared by use of the 'taking into consideration' (tic) procedure. The authors note that for all offence groups combined in their sample, one quarter of offences regarded by the police as being cleared up were dealt with in this way. Unfortunately, Steer gives little attention to this important aspect of investigation, a fact which undoubtedly contributes considerably to the rather more optimistic view of police investigatory skill to be drawn from his report.

On the basis of evidence from American and British studies, there can be little doubt that the detection and clearance of the commoner forms of crime depends for the most part upon the willingness and ability of the public to report criminal incidents to the police. Unfortunately, in their eagerness to make this point, authors, perhaps with the exception of Steer, have failed to

32

draw on their research to identify those areas within which police skills may play some part. The detective has a variety of skills. These include gathering information from the public; locating suspects; interviewing and, on the basis of information derived from both the public and suspects, of preparing cases for the prosecution. On the question of 'tic' clearances at present it is not apparent from the literature how much importance should be attached to these. Some authors suggest that the police contribute nothing to clearances of this nature. Possibly, however, it would be more realistic to regard 'tic' clearances as the tip of an iceberg of police work which has been underway for several months. At present the former view prevails — at least, that is, outside of police circles.

7 Constraints on policing

From the preceding chapters there seems little doubt that despite their tactical orientation to crime control, policemen spend a large part of their time responding to demands for service which subsequently are not defined as criminal incidents. Meantime, as the volume of recorded crime continues to rise, the ability of the police to control it becomes a matter of increasing controversy. Some (notably serving police officers) suggest that the explanation is to be found in a lack of resources allocated to the police, the legal constraints within which the police operate and the ambiguity of the law. Others draw attention to what they regard as the organisational weakness of the police service (Holdaway, 1977), and the ambivalence of public attitudes both towards the police and towards criminal behaviour (Shaw and Williamson, 1972). These constraints are discussed in this chapter. But as noted earlier the principal constraint on effective policing stems from the nature of crime itself. This point emerges clearly from several of the studies discussed in this review and must, as noted in Chapter 9, be taken into account in planning further research on the police.

Economic constraints

The argument that the effectiveness of the police is principally constrained by a lack of resources finds little or no support in the research literature. Indeed, as noted in Chapter 4, most studies based on aggregate data indicate that rather than reducing crime, increased expenditure on the police service is frequently accompanied, as a result of the 'reporting phenomena', by increases in the levels of crime reported. Similarly, studies of police patrol and CID branches provide no indications that the effectiveness of either can readily be improved by increasing manpower.

Several authors have noted that since the second world war the level of recorded crime has continued to rise both in this country and abroad despite rapid increases in the size of police services. Hough (1980), for example, reports that the combined police and civilian establishments of provincial forces in England and Wales have risen by about 150% since the war. Moreover in questioning the accuracy of popular belief, Hough suggests that there are at present more rather than less uniformed officers patrolling the streets than in the early post-war years. Writing of Canadian and American policing, Engstad and Evans (1980) present a similar picture noting that "it is now apparent that despite massive increases in police personnel and equipment the magnitude and seriousness of the crime problem has not abated".

Several reasons have been put forward to explain why gains in economic resources have not been translated into increased police effectiveness in controlling crime, and some of the principal constraints impinging upon the police are discussed in this chapter. Before considering these, however, it is necessary to raise two further points regarding the nature of economic expenditure. First it is apparent that the relationship between expenditure on the police and crime control is at best complex. Indeed it is the absence of a 'common sense' relationship that has encouraged some police officers, police administrators and others to look to other factors constraining the effectiveness of the police. Second, while a matter for speculation, it has been argued that expenditure on the police *may* have already reached an optimum level (Alderson, 1979) and that as a result the allocation of further resources would result in a little more than marginal gains on the control of crime. If additional funds are spent to procure 'more of the same' policing then the research literature supports Alderson's view. The only qualification to this view would arise if, in the unlikely event police financial resources quadrupled, the ratio of police officers to public rose dramatically. Given that only a small proportion of the public are criminally active, the ratio of police officers to criminals would be considerably higher. However, such measures, assuming they were feasible, would almost certainly result in police activity encroaching not only on the liberty of criminals but also on that of the public at large. Under these circumstances the social and economic costs of living with crime might be considerably less than the costs of attempting to eliminate it.

Legal constraints

The constraints imposed on policing by the limitations of police powers are more difficult to disentangle and assess. Any account must acknowledge, on the one hand, the limitations of police powers and the legal protection offered to the citizen which, on occasions may impede police effectiveness, and, on the other, the opportunities open to the police to circumvent the law.

Since it is undoubtedly true that in certain areas police powers are limited[1] it is surprising that the impact of these upon police performance has been almost totally disregarded by research. There are a number of reasons for this. Steer (1980) suggests that with some notable exceptions (e.g. Stinchombe, 1963) researchers have little knowledge of the legal powers of the police or the procedures followed by them, and as a result, have failed to take them into account. Moreover, as far as American policing is concerned the subject is only of limited importance since the task of the detective is solely to apprehend the suspect and not, as with his British counterpart, to bring the suspect to trial.

---

[1] Whitaker (1979) notes, for example, that except in motoring and Official Secrets Act cases a person questioned by the police is under no legal obligation to supply his identity or address. Similarly, a member of the public unless formally arrested, is not obliged to comply with a request to accompany a police officer to the police station.

In view of this omission, it is of particular interest that Steer's recent work on the reporting and investigation of crime considers, if only briefly, the subject of legal constraints. Writing of a small sample of suspects whom the police had reasonable grounds to arrest, but for lack of evidence were unable to charge, Steer concludes that:

> . . . from the evidence in the study there are no obvious powers which the police might have that would greatly enhance their effectiveness in the detection of crime.

However, Steer also notes that it should be recognised that:

> . . . the interviewing of persons arrested plays an essential part in the discovery and more importantly in the detection of crime, and that the restriction of powers in this area could lead to a dramatic fall in the detection rate.

There is of course a second characteristic to be considered regarding the powers of the police, namely that being nowhere properly defined their limits are uncertain. Within these ambiguities lies the opportunity for the police to circumvent the law and for the courts to reinterpret the law, both activities serving to reduce the constraining impact of the law upon police behaviour. Several authors (e.g. Skolnick, 1966) have noted that in a system which on the one hand limits the powers of the police, while on the other demands high performance in terms, for example, of arrest, it is inevitable that rules are "bent" to achieve operational objectives: the process Skolnick has described as an "occupational necessity". Moreover, McBarnet (1979) argues this is a process which is condoned by others within the criminal justice system. She concludes:

> It is not just the police who informally point to the practical needs for crime control to justify ignoring the principles of legality, the same principle is writ large and indeed offered as guidance for the police in cases, text books and government reports which formulate the law itself.

The origins and consequences of extra-legal activity are difficult to identify and assess. Cain (1979) has noted that for many concerned with research into civil rights and police powers, problems, including corruption, are seen to stem largely from the activities of a few "bad" people within the organisation. By this argument problems will be resolved by the removal of such people. An alternative and more probable explanation, and one expressed by a number of writers (Cox, *et al.,* 1977; Skolnick, 1966; Goldstein, 1975) is that corruption is a product of police organisation and the nature of the task the police undertake. Other writers (cf. Goldstein, 1975) have pointed out that as many laws are difficult to enforce, and thus non-enforcement common the legislature itself provides the opportunity for the public to buy immunity, and for the police to take or withhold action for profit. Given this view, it can be argued that corruption is inevitable (Whyte, 1955; Wilson, 1968) and that the type of professionalism that might control corruption would, by its rigidity, prejudice police effectiveness. Whatever the case, it seems likely that the overall effect of corruption will be to the disadvantage of the community since, at a general level, the law itself falls into disrepute when those who enforce it are found to be corrupt (Holdaway, 1979). At the more practical level of police management, where the behaviour of an officer is controlled by payment outside of the force to which he belongs, the formal organisational control system fails to work; similarly, where an officer spends his time in corrupt activities, his inclinations to carry out police duties are curtailed (Goldstein, 1975). There are grounds for arguing, therefore, that where limitations of police powers lead to extra-legal police activities, such activities will, in the long run, be prejudicial to the effectiveness of the service in controlling crime.

Organisational constraints

It has long been recognised that one of the principal constraints upon the effectiveness of policing arises from the nature of the organisation within which the police officer works. The nub of the problem is to find an organisational structure which allows monitoring and control without prejudicing quality of performance.

Angell (1971) has argued that concepts of centralised authority and responsibility, being fundamental to the traditional bureaucracy, are found in most police departments and that their presence is prejudicial to police community relations. In his view, centralised departmental structure encourages the development of inflexible policies which, in failing to recognise the needs of minority groups within the community, hinder the development of sound police relations with those groups. Similarly, the notions of centralised power and decision-making discourage active involvement with the community which, in time, leads many citizens to regard the police department as being beyond their control and understanding. Not infrequently these problems are exacerbated by the mode of communication found in many police departments which, relying on the traditional supervisor/subordinate relationship, can easily distort and filter information passing from one officer to the next. Tullock (1965) presents a similar picture. As a result, many directives issued by senior officers (which as a result of the process of distortion may well themselves be formed on the basis of inaccurate information) will not infrequently be misinterpreted as they travel down the rank structure, and so fail to have the impact originally intended.

For the British police system at least, constraints created by the bureaucratic organisation have to some extent been strengthened by the considerable autonomy enjoyed by the lower ranks whose working ethos is at odds with that of their superiors. Thus Holdaway (1977) has pointed to a duality of professionalism within the police service: managerial professionalism sponsoring quiet observational methods, a slow build-up of evidence preparatory to arrest and, if one accepts the view of Cain (1972), the development of a more responsible norm towards the community, and the emergence of an effective

37

form of self-policing for the community. By contrast, for junior ranks, professionalism embraces the crime-fighting image of the police and favours "hedonistic, protective and highly practical initiatives and values which are largely opposed to those of managerial professionalism" (Holdaway, 1977).

The practical consequences of this schism are most clearly illustrated in a paper by James (1979) in which the author considers the important question of black/police relations. The paper reports the formation of a crime squad to arrest offenders (principally black youths) responsible for thefts from the person and robbery in a particular area. The research shows how junior officers allocated to the squad (itself based on the tenets of managerial professionalism) manage first to gain freedom from the control of senior officers and to establish control over their work, and so redefine the objectives handed down to them. As a result of the squads' increasing autonomy, communication between the ranks was impaired and the broad objectives of eradicating social discrimination frustrated. Moreover, the objectives of policing within the rule of law and bringing long term solutions to bear on the police/immigrant problem gave way to extra-legal tactics in a bid to gain evidence and make swift arrests.

There is some support for the view, therefore, that the development of managerial professionalism within the service, which in this country *may* have lessened the constraints imposed by the organisational structure of policing, has been hampered by the unique position of the junior ranks. These officers, by virtue of their common law status and nature of their work, maintain an independence from senior officers and develop their own working ethos. The difficulty of attempting to counteract the influence of this group stems from their autonomy and ability to control the information (Chatterton, 1976). Moreover, the norms subscribed to by junior ranks have been established to counter the boredom, unpleasantness and frustration of much of the work junior officers are obliged to undertake.

A recent paper by Goldstein (1979) draws attention to a second constraint arising from the organisation of policing, namely that associated with the "means over ends" syndrome common to most police departments. Writing of North American policing, Goldstein notes that while much attention has been given to improving the organisation of operating methods, little interest is usually shown in the *substantive* output of the department's work. Engstadt and Evans (1980) confirm this view with regard to Canadian policing. Historically, the development of British and Canadian policing is dissimilar, but there can be little doubt that in many police forces an administrative style, stressing the process of regulation and a maintenance of the organisation — manifest in the plethora of internal regulations affecting the day-to-day running of the police — has prevailed. As a consequence of this, a managerial perspective — which might place greater emphasis on ensuring that the goals of the organisation were both viable and attained — has been slow to emerge. In the absence of this, the police have tended to accept as the objectives of their organisation the tasks others have ascribed to them. Indeed, as Manning (1977) has noted for American policing, historically such a process has been welcomed by the police as a way of securing public recognition of the police service. The costs of such a process are, of course, the accumulation of a range of responsibilities, the fulfilment of which lies beyond the capability of the service.

Police/public attitudes

Since the inception of the police service it has been recognised as essential for the police to secure the co-operation of the public. Where hostility arises between the police and the community the task of policing becomes immeasurably more difficult (Ignatieff, 1979). For the most part surveys conducted both in this country and the United States have shown the public to be almost universally satisfied with the police and the service they offer, (Government Social Survey, 1962; Belson, 1978; Hindelang *et al.*, 1975). These findings may present, however, an over simplified view of the situation since the police themselves perceive public confidence to be declining, and their relations with the public deteriorating (Thomas and Hyman, 1977; Banton, 1974; Cain, 1977). One way to make sense of these contradictory findings is to distinguish between public attitudes to the police as an institution, and their attitudes to the behaviour of the police of whom they have first hand experience. For the most part, surveys of the public have concentrated on the police as an institution. As a result the general expressions of satisfaction which characterise so much of this work, both in England and elsewhere, may simply reflect people's acceptance of the legitimacy of the police, their rights and duties and indeed the necessity for the police. However, where studies have directed the public to answer specific questions (as applied to *your* police rather than *the* police) higher rates of dissatisfaction have been revealed (Courtis *et al.*, 1970; Kelling *et al.*, 1974; Reiss *et al.*, 1967).

Shaw and Williamson (1972), reporting on the findings of a British survey, commented on wide variation in attitudes towards the police held by members of the public living in different areas (within the same city), from different social classes and from different age groups. The authors note that it is not simply:

> ...a question of more favourable attitudes emanating from those with better housing, higher levels of income, better life chances etc. .... it is that people in those categories have been stopped and questioned less often, and that there is a clear and direct connection between adverse attitudes to the police and hostile contact with them.

The study underscores, therefore, the importance of differentiating between general and particular attitudes and of recognising the importance of the part played by the police in shaping the latter.

The obverse but equally important side of the coin is considered by Thomas and Hyman (1977) who, in a study based on data gathered by postal question-naires, consider the accuracy with which the police perceive their relationship with the public. The principal conclusions of the study are noted below:

i. Police images of public apathy towards them are largely the product of their selected contacts with special categories of the public who, for a variety of reasons, (they are black, young, less affluent, reside in inner city areas etc.) are less than favourable in their reactions. This obser-vation adds weight to findings of public opinion studies (Hindelang *et al.,* 1975) which all stressed that unfavourable attitudes to the police are to be found amongst those in particular groups.

ii. Police efforts which seek to foster a more favourable public relations programme are either of little benefit or redundant.

iii. Police departmental efforts could more advantageously be directed towards altering their own perceptions, since the police themselves may play an important role in fostering antipathy amongst those who have unfavourable evaluations by virtue of their responses to these categories of citizens.

These conclusions are important for two reasons. First, they suggest that the perceptions held by the police not only weaken relations between the police and the community, but are likely to encourage the police to over-react to particular situations — a point made by Smith and Hawkins (1973) and Berkley *et al.,* (1976). Second, the police perceptions of the public's attitude towards them leads to the present emphasis on changing the non-police population rather than the police. This, McDowell (1971) argues, is to misconceive the situation since the public respond to the way in which the police choose to deal with them. McDowell notes:

Stickers that enjoin citizens to support their local police and little league baseball teams sponsored by police units are commendable efforts, but they are nevertheless roads which lead nowhere. To change the image, the police must change themselves.

McDowell questions why the police should look like a private army, complete with rank structure and terminology, and suggests that such an image projects the right of the police to exercise the lawful force of the state "in an often far from subtle manner". Consequently, the author continues, many people shun the police just to be on the safe side and, "the most tragic result of this is that many young men who are thus attracted to the police as a profession look forward to being a figure who commands fear".

It would of course be an over simplification to suggest that police expectations of public hostility are solely the result of unfavourable contacts with relatively small sections of the public. Whitaker (1964) and Cain (1973) have both pointed to the difficulties of the police task and the lack of recognition they receive for it. Punch (1979) observes that by comparison with many other occupations police work does not demand high entry standards or prolonged training. These characteristics, which themselves reflect the mundane nature of much routine police work, must, in Punch's view, play a part in reinforcing the police officer's low self esteem.

Of the constraints considered in this chapter the most important arise from the nature of the police organisation and police relationships with the public — two aspects of policing which are considered further in the concluding chapters of this review.

8 Community policing

The research reviewed in the preceding chapters suggests that the constraints on traditional methods of policing impose fairly close limits upon effectiveness. Moreover, although some modest successes are reported for the more innovative styles of specialist policing, the unintended and often prejudicial consequences of specialisation, both within the force and on community relations, have frequently been overlooked.

When the traditional strategies of a service are seen to be less than successful it is not uncommon to seek solutions within the community. This has been true of a number of organisations including those concerned with social work, provision for the mentally ill and the treatment of offenders. The process is usually cyclical; when the community is found to be less supportive than originally believed there is a move back towards a belief in centralisation and specialisation. There are signs that the police service may be following at least the first part of this trend, for in recent years much interest has been expressed in the value of community policing. The definitional problems relating to this concept are severe, and in the following pages the term 'community policing' is taken to refer to a process whereby responsibility for the control of crime within the community is shared between the police and the public. The term 'preventive policing' is not employed in this chapter on the grounds that all work undertaken by the police can legitimately be subsumed under this heading.

Parkinson (1977) has suggested that the most significant aspect of community policing consists in breaking down the barriers separating the community and the police:

> Police departments have begun to move towards a variety of forms of policing ... in which they attempt to redefine their own role in the community, to establish new and more helpful relations with the community, and to act as a catalyst to involve other professions and citizens in sharing the responsibility for things which have been seen as a problem for the police alone.

If interpreted in this broad manner, community policing may be the most fruitful means of fulfilling the wide variety of tasks presently falling to the police. However, it is a view predicated upon the belief that communities exist which share similar values to the police, and whose members are capable of self-regulation through the development of police/community relations.

Kelling (1978), for example, refers to "normal social control exercised by healthy communities", and stresses the need for improved police/community interaction both in terms of quality and quantity.

This presents problems of a theoretical and practical nature. First, much of the discussion of community policing has tended to overlook the politically ambivalent role the concept poses for the police; the resolution of a particular conflict may well be to the satisfaction of one group in the community at the expense of another, a point that is particularly pertinent in the case of minority groups. Similarly, while they may be perceived as involved in community relations work, the police may in practice be actively engaged in social control (Parnas, 1971; Gelles, 1972).

The second difficulty arises from the fact that a belief in community policing assumes a romantic version of society involving "the return to some arcadian existence where (crime)...is kept in check by the local community, that is by the commonality of ordinary people" (Croft, 1979). A few countries may, because of their cultural and economic characteristics, be particularly suited to a form of policing in which the community, aided by the police, controls crime. Japan provides an obvious example, (Bayley, 1976). However, most of the population of Europe and North America live in a highly differentiated society where as Banton (1978) has noted:

> In the anonymity of the city street, the factory, and the market place, the opportunities for crime are multiplied ... social and geographical mobility have created relationships that cannot be governed by informal controls.

The high degree of individualism which characterises most western societies stands as a major constraint likely to limit the effectiveness of any form of policing which relies heavily on the collective endeavours of the community. Moreover, only where groups are homogeneous and well organised are they able to establish relationships with the police, and to respond to police initiatives. This may explain the fact that in some areas of Britain senior police officers currently claim success in community policing on the grounds that they are responding to a community, which itself is organised to the extent that it can request the police to 'move in'. It should be recognised, however, that in such situations the police are not necessarily responding to the community as a whole, but to leaders or small groups whose representativeness is always open to doubt.

A third obstacle to the development of community policing arises when crime control requires collaboration between the police and other agencies in the community. Here problems can arise regarding the sharing of information between agencies, the accountability of different agencies and their respective responsibilities. That these problems can be overcome has been demonstrated by the work of the crime prevention support unit of the Devon and Cornwall constabulary (cf. Blaber, 1979), and the police/social work experiment in Illinois, monitored by Treger (1980). Such efforts, however, rest on the view that it is within the capacity of the public to control crime and that they are willing to work in co-operation with the police. While this may be true, at least in part, too little attempt has been made to examine the crime control capability of the public and the various ways in which the police might encourage and sustain public co-operation.

Given the diversity of community policing schemes now in existence, it is unlikely that much will be gained by attempting rigorous classification. Yet between the more important community policing activities — the deployment of area constables, increased co-operation between the police and local authority agencies (particularly schools and social service departments), the introduction of team policing, and the development of so-called 'situational' policing — discernible differences can be detected.

Taking first the more modest exercises (at least in terms of their organisation) much interest has been expressed in the use of area constables, community constables or home beat officers as a means to narrow the gap between the police and the community. In general it is argued that improvements will result in police/public attitudes; in the flow of information between the police and the public; in public fear of crime and ultimately in the level of crime itself.

Although much effort has been devoted to community policing in this country (cf. Alderson, 1979; Knights, 1980) to date remarkably little empirical research has been carried out — most studies having done little more than provide detailed description of police activities (Blaber, 1979; Schaffer, 1980), or examine the problems arising when officers are re-deployed from traditional forms of policing to community policing activities (Pullé, 1973; James, 1979).

One exception, the work of a serving police officer, Pollard (1979), evaluated a community policing experiment in the Highfields area of Leicestershire. Constables involved with the experiment were given responsibility for policing a designated area and a general remit to establish a firm relationship with members of the community and so create "an atmosphere within the environment in which the community is more able and willing to regulate itself". The evaluation of the experiment relied largely on qualitative data. However, interviews with the police indicated that, in their view at least, the flow of information from the public about criminal activity increased as the public became better acquainted with local officers. As far as the residents were concerned Pollard reports that the majority of those interviewed felt "more secure and confident" as a result of the introduction of the community scheme. In another study, undertaken by Manolias (1980) in Gainsborough, it was again found that the introduction of a community scheme increased the flow of information between the public and the police regarding criminal activities, particularly the activities of juveniles. This occurred, Manolias records, as a result of the links forged with the public through a school liaison scheme.

Many police forces in attempting to draw closer to the community have attempted to improve the degree of collaboration between police officers and members of other local authority agencies. Liaison has probably been most successful with regard to schools and local education departments. In broad terms school liaison schemes are designed to inculcate in pupils an understanding of the role of the police and a respect for law and order, as well as to alert the pupils to the need for crime prevention. In practice, some schemes amount to little more than a formal lecture given by a police officer on, for example, road safety. But in others police officers are actively involved in teaching examination curricula and organising extra-mural activities.

No firm evidence is available regarding the effectiveness of these schemes which probably can only be fully evaluated over a long period of time (cf. Pollard, 1979). In the short term, however, such schemes may be of value in improving relations between children (particularly young children) and the police, and there is some evidence that the intitial hostility of ethnic minorities has been successfully countered by police efforts (Manolias, 1980).

A second aspect of liaison with local education departments takes the form of 'truancy' patrols. In an experiment conducted in Bristol, patrol teams, consisting of a uniformed police officer and an education welfare officer, patrolled a central shopping precinct and an outlying housing estate (Ekblom, 1979). The patrol stopped and recorded the age and sex of all unaccompanied children and noted any reasons offered for absence from school. The study suggested relatively little daylight crime was committed by children and, that on balance, the patrol played little part in the reduction of truancy in the experimental area. The author also makes the point, however, that patrols organised on a rather larger scale and supported by some form of welfare provision for the truants returned to school, may well lead to a reduction in the number of children on the street during school hours in localities where truancy was known to be high.

A further category of community policing activities are those concerned with 'team' or 'zone' policing. This form of policing is probably the most thoroughly evaluated of the range of community activities discussed in this chapter. Although diversity exists betwen the various team policing experiments described in the literature, where "community-based" the approach, "has evolved into a truly fundamental departure from the traditional police field service" (Edgar et al., 1976). In general the concept of team policing is an attempt to strike a balance between the presumed needs of police centralisation, and the advantages of decentralisation in terms of responsiveness to the public. The basic organisational elements of team policing are geographical stability of patrol, decentralisation of authority, and maximum communication amongst team members and with members of the community (Sherman et al., 1973; Wasson, 1975). Typically, where community-based, teams comprise a senior supervisor, several junior supervisors, and sufficient officers to provide at least the basic police services to a designated neighbourhood on a 24-hour-a-day basis. The team determines its own deployment, working hours, shift assignments and schedules, and method of operation within broad police guidelines established by the department. In organisational terms, if nothing else, team policing amounts to a considerably broader and more complex approach to community policing than the schemes described above.

Evaluations undertaken to assess the effect of this form of policing provide tentative evidence that the introduction of team policing leads to an increase in the amount of information made available to the police by members of the community, to improvements in police/public relations, and to a reduction in the level of reported crime (O'Malley, 1973; Schwartz, et al., 1974; Angell, 1975). These advantages, however, can only be achieved at the cost of considerable reorganisation in the way in which policing is managed.

Nilsson (1980), working in collaboration with the Gothenburg police, evaluated the preliminary stage of a team policing project which was completed in the spring of 1979. During the experiment five teams were created (each team comprised two patrolmen and one detective) as a result of which a 50% increase occurred in the number of patrol officers deployed in the experimental area. Statistically significant reductions were found to have occurred with regard to all aspects of crime. However, with the exception of calls for service, the reduction was matched by an increase in crime in an adjacent area. Moreover, after the experiment was concluded and the teams disbanded, the level of crime rose in the area to the level preceding the experiment. Nilsson concludes that the experiment caused displacement of crime; that the team concept worked well in improving job motivation and satisfaction; but that despite the increase in resources and improved organisation the effects of the experiment were of limited magnitude and duration.

Sherman et al., (1973), on reviewing seven team policing experiments conducted in North America reaches the view that: "It would be tempting to conclude that team policing had certain consequences for crime, community relations, and police morale and productivity. The data are far too scant, however, to make such conclusions final". Sherman notes, however, that the limitations of team policing lie, not in the weakness of the method, but in the organisational difficulties encountered in its implementation. In particular Sherman comments on the hostility of middle management within police departments, and the weakness of deployment policies which did not permit patrol officers attached to the teams to remain in their areas. It is clear, therefore, that any future attempt to evaluate team policing must take steps to resolve the practical and organisational problems likely to impede the effectiveness of this form of policing.

The development of community policing has of course run alongside, and, to some extent, cut across the traditional interest of the police in preventing crime through physical crime prevention techniques (locks, safety-chains, strong rooms, security glass and vehicle intruder alarms). This approach to prevention fits more easily into the police ethos given the notion of 'real police work', and finds some support in a recent report prepared by police officers (A.C.P.O., 1979) which refers to "the need for the Crime Prevention Centre (a Home Office training establishment) to concentrate on the physical aspects of crime prevention". The two approaches are clearly dissimilar: community policing, a liberal concept which is difficult to operationalise, and physical crime prevention — a constraining activity, but one easy to implement. In recent years, however, a third approach has been developed which, by combining elements of both community policing and physical crime prevention, may well offer a more promising strategy (Mayhew *et al.,* 1976; Ley and Cybriwsky, 1974; Heywood, 1979; Clarke, 1980; Clarke and Mayhew, 1980). In brief this work involves analysis of the situational context in which different crimes are committed and, on the basis of this information, attempts to change the situation so making crime more difficult to commit for the 'opportunistic' offender, and more hazardous for professional criminals by increasing their chances of apprehension.

In that the 'situational' approach to crime encourages close police liaison with other agencies in the community, it shares a number of important characteristics with the more traditional approaches to community policing described above. However, in that crime is seen as the outcome of an offender's response to the characteristics of particular situations, the approach is unimpeded by the belief that a community, under enlightened leadership, will have both the inclination and capacity to sustain enduring control over its members. The 'situational' perspective provides, therefore, yet another way in which community policing might develop. Engstad and Evans (1980), drawing on the work of Heywood (1979), have linked the idea of crime analysis with the notion of community responsibility for crime to provide something of a conceptual basis and empirical foundation for the evaluation of what might be called 'situational policing'. They argue that crime problems have traditionally been analysed, and "crime attack" strategies formulated, "without careful questioning of who in the community was responsible, to what extent, for the existence or control of specific crimes, thus restricting the search for alternative responses to crime problems". The alternative response which Engstad and Evans envisage is that the police should make a conscious attempt to shift the focus of responsibility for crime control to the community. They suggest that the concept of responsibility provides the basis for examining key aspects of the role and functions of the police in crime control. This involves the following steps:

i. The location of trouble-spots in an area, and an analysis of the necessary prerequisites for incidents to occur (such as presence of potential offenders, opportunity for offending and lack of surveillance). This work will include the identification of those in the community who, either individually or collectively, contribute to crime by creating opportunities for offences to occur, or by failing to take responsible action.

47

ii. Planning ways to reduce the situational inducements to criminal behaviour and to block environmental opportunities.

iii. The implementation of plans. This will involve the transfer of the responsibility for the control of specific crime problems to members of the community (individuals, assorted agencies, institutions), and to finding ways of ensuring that those concerned take appropriate action.

Whilst it is not uncommon for community policing schemes to invoke the support of the populace in general (as with police open-days and exhortations to assist the police), in the form of policing proposed, the police single out a group of individuals or particular organisations indicating how they may be contributing to the problem and requesting their co-operation to alleviate it.

The preceding discussion has shown community policing to have a number of different objectives. At the simplest level it is the community constable's job to encourage favourable attitudes on the part of the public, thereby helping the police, adopting conventional tactics, to control crime. An alternative perspective is that it is the task of the police officer, acting as a catalyst within the community, to encourage the public to share responsibility for crime and to co-operate actively with the police in keeping it in check. Clearly this is a considerably broader remit, and one which stems from the view that the effectiveness of the police, when working in isolation from the community, is severely limited. The final chapter of this review argues that one of the principal tasks of future research is to identify ways in which police and public can work together to control crime.

9 Future research

Views differ regarding the current state of police research. On the one hand it can be argued that now that the second or third 'round' of research has been completed, results can be synthesised and future research strategies planned with confidence. Others take a more pessimistic view, arguing that past research has been both fragmentary and superficial and what is needed is not a "synthesis of what we know, but rather a synthesis...of what we do not know" (Kelling *et al.*, 1980). While neither view is entirely satisfactory, particularly for a British audience forced to rely largely on North American literature, past research has undoubtedly challenged the popular image of the police (Clarke & Hough, 1980). At the risk of some over-simplification the message most obviously to be drawn from this review is that it is beyond the ability of the police to have a direct effect on a good deal of crime.

There are a number of responses to this message: it can be argued, for example, that research underpinning the conclusion is itself wrong; that the objectives pursued by the police are inappropriate; and/or that police tactics designed to achieve these objectives are unsuitable. Certainly all of the studies discussed in this review are open to varying degrees of criticism: problems of crime displacement, maintenance of adequate control groups, and the measurement of police performance impinge to a lesser or greater extent upon every research undertaking. Even if some replication of earlier studies may be necessary, the cumulative evidence from completed studies, whatever their individual weaknesses, is, nevertheless, remarkably consistent in supporting the view that few police tactics seem to work very well. Moreover, and perhaps of greater importance, now that more information is coming to hand regarding crime and its characteristics, it is becoming clearer why many tactics are not achieving their desired objectives.

Alternatively, it might be claimed that some recently developed technological aids, particularly computers, have greatly enhanced the capacity of the police to control crime, and that as a consequence the findings of past research can best be regarded as of historical interest. In practice, however, the value of technology to the police has probably been over-emphasised. Kelling (1978) has observed that with few exceptions "there is no evidence that any technological devices have significantly improved the effectiveness of the police service". Other critics of technological innovation generally see new devices as being, at worst, expensive 'toys', but Kelling argues that the problem is more serious in so far as technological innovation in policing can result in a deterioration in the quality of service received by the public.

There are no doubt some areas where technology can facilitate police work. Hough (1980), for example, while critical of early attempts to develop 'command and control' and 'management information' systems, notes that computers may have some limited part to play in areas of criminal investigation work and traffic policing. While this may be so, and similar conclusions, at least with regard to criminal investigation, can be drawn from other authors (Bloch and Bell, 1976; Greenwood *et al.*, 1977; Boyston, 1975) there is little ground for arguing that technological innovation in policing should constitute a primary focus for future research effort. There are, as this review has shown, a number of more fundamental issues to be explored, notably the objectives of policing and the characteristics of tactics adopted to achieve these objectives. Before considering these, however, it is useful to raise, and so clear from the discussion, two important but subsidiary methodological points regarding the assessment of police performance.

The first concerns the tendency on the part of researchers to rely on official crime statistics in evaluating police activity. Some official figures are no doubt more reliable than others (Bottomley and Coleman, 1980), but there remains ample scope for error, bias, and misinformation to make the interpretation equivocal of any research evaluation based solely on official rates of reported crime. One aspect of the problem can be illustrated by reference to the evaluation of community policing experiments where police success in breaking down the barriers between the police and the public may well lead to increases in the level of officially recorded crime (Laugharne, 1980).

One way of getting round these difficulties is by the use of victim surveys of people in target areas or, in some cases, by the use of self-report measures of criminal activity. While costly to use, many of the methodological flaws attached to earlier victimisation and self-report studies have now been overcome (cf. Sparks *et al.*, 1977; Skogan, 1976). Both methods offer an opportunity to record the level of criminality in an area and, by avoiding problems associated with 'reporting phenomena', of assessing the impact of police activity in controlling and preventing criminal behaviour. On occasions it may also be possible to assess police performance by more direct methods. For example, in a study designed to assess the effectiveness of a police organised publicity campaign aimed to reduce auto-crime, doors and windows of vehicles were physically checked to see whether a change in the level of security occurred during the campaign (Burrows and Heal, 1979). Similarly, in a study designed to assess the effectiveness of truancy patrols, counts were made during school hours of the number of children wandering the streets in a patrol area (Ekblom, 1979).

The second point concerns the possibility of the displacement of crime following a change in police activity; this may come about as a result of offenders shifting their activity to other locations, or to other types of crime. There are therefore two aspects to this question. First, on the assumption that crime is susceptible to police presence, it might be argued that police activity in an area will displace crime to adjacent districts. Nilsson (1980), describing a team policing experiment in Gothenburg reports such a result.

It is likely, however, that on many occasions the phenomenon of displacement is more complex than ititially appears (Chaiken, 1978; Clarke, 1980): much will depend on the nature of crime occurring and the characteristics of would-be offenders. Thus displacement is most likely when the crime occurring in an area is such that it can be committed in one area as well as the next, and when those responsible for the crime can themselves move freely to adjacent areas. On the other hand, crimes associated with the characteristics (social or physical) of an area, and committed by those with limited opportunity to move away from that area, are less likely to be displaced. Thus 'joy-riding' in stolen cars, incidents associated with street disturbance and some aspects of vandalism which were committed, for example, by juveniles living in and, to some extent, confined to a public housing estate are unlikely to be displaced by police activity.

The second aspect of the displacement argument rests on the view that the successful prevention of one type of crime leads to the commission of another. Implicit in this argument is the assumption (now increasingly discredited) that crime is committed by people with a propensity to criminal behaviour which will be expressed in one form or another. This view is challenged in a recent paper by Clarke (1980) in which it is argued that traditional criminological theory in placing emphasis on criminal disposition ignores the importance of the situation in which crime occurs, and fails to see crime as an immediate outcome of choices and decisions made by the offender. In developing this argument Clarke suggests that a great deal of crime is committed by people who would not ordinarily be thought of as 'criminal' and is heavily influenced by the inducements of the situation and the balance of risks and rewards involved.

Although changes in policing may not always result in the displacement of all crimes, unless research is designed to take account of the possibility of displacement, results obtained in evaluating police activities will remain equivocal.

Police objectives
Many researchers concerned with the criminal justice system have in recent years devoted much effort to considering the role and objectives of the police. In the broadest terms there are two schools of thought. First, it can be argued that the police should primarily be concerned with the control of crime and enforcement of law. Morris *et al.*, (1977) have argued, for example, that the criminal justice system should be reorganised so that the police would deal primarily with violent and predatory crimes, eschewing responsibility for social service calls. Responsibility for controlling a range of activities such as vandalism, bribery, possession of stolen property, gambling and acts contrary to public decency would then fall primarily upon civilian agents and

inspectors. Undoubtedly such an approach would enable the police to devote all of their resources to 'real crime'. However, a problem arises as to whether the police actually know what to do with the free time made available to them (Sweeney and Illingsworth, 1973). An alternative approach is that the police should devote their efforts and resources primarily to keeping the peace and to the service of the community. Unfortunately it is unlikely that either this approach or that proposed by Morris would be particularly helpful. A more practical course is to review the crime control tasks traditionally ascribed to the police, and to sort those that are feasible from those falling beyond the capability of the police to achieve.

This apparently simple task, which might be seen as being the primary focus for future research, is beset with problems. On the one hand, public debate, drawing heavily on the mythology of police effectiveness, perpetuates a series of time-honoured, if artificial, objectives for the service to achieve; on the other, the incredibly broad range of incidents brought to the attention of the police encourages the police to continually diversify their activities. Arguably the effectiveness of the service can only be improved if the objectives of policing are determined not by public demand and debate but by a process which, while reflecting the needs of the public, takes account not only of the unique powers of the police, but also the constraints likely to impinge upon police performance. Of these, the most powerful is undoubtedly the nature of crime itself.

Setting aside the difficulties likely to be encountered by research, some preliminary, if tentative, views can be put forward as to the type of tasks associated with the control of crime that police might set out to achieve. Five tasks, working from the most general to the particular (there may well be others) are noted below:

i. The police have a responsibility for alleviating the community's fear of crime which in practice may be only loosely related to the actual level of crime occurring, and is possibly more socially harmful.

ii. While the police may be unable to catch an offender, the responsibility remains to support the victim for whom the aftermath of the incident may well be more distressing than the incident itself.

iii. It is possible that crimes could be reduced if the public acted in a more intelligent way when crime occurred. If this is so, it is clearly the responsibility of the police to educate the public how to avoid criminal incidents where possible, or where they do occur, how best to respond to them.

iv. The police have an important role to play intervening in situations about to fall beyond the control of individual members of the public, and to do so in such a way as to prevent criminal incidents occurring, for example, domestic disputes, rowdyism in the streets.

52

v. Within the broad category of incidents reported, it is likely that some crimes, because of their particular characteristics, could be curtailed by police activity. It falls to the police to identify these crimes and to develop appropriate tactics in an attempt to control them.

Each of the tasks listed above constitutes an important aspect of police work, and as such warrants careful study. But for many people the principal responsibility of the police will remain the control of recorded crime, and there is therefore a case for regarding the last of the five tasks listed as forming the primary focus of research activity over the next few years. Research in this area would involve the identification of offences likely to be curtailed by the police, and the evaluation of appropriate tactics — three of which are discussed in the final section of this review.

Police tactics
Of the tactics at their disposal police have made most use of those they regard as controlling a range of different types of crimes — patrolling provides an obvious example. It is possible that this may be an important reason for the limited success attributed to traditional policing, and that 'crime specific' tactics, that is tactics designed to control carefully delineated forms of criminal behaviour, would be more successful. This view might be taken as a guideline for those planning future research into the effectiveness of policing, as it is possible to identify within the principal areas of police work a number of crime specific activities. Three examples are discussed below: case screening procedures; specialisation, particularly in patrolling; and 'situational' policing.

i. Case screening procedures
A better understanding of the characteristics of crime would undoubtedly enhance the development of case-screening techniques to select solvable from unsolvable crime at a very early stage in the investigatory process. Research has shown that "solvability" factors can be identified, and that where these are used to direct resources to particularly serious crimes or to those crimes which, because of the circumstances within which they occur, are likely to be solved by investigation, much wasted effort can be saved (Bloch and Bell, 1976; Bloch and Weidman, 1975). Many criminal investigation departments in this country already make some use of screening techniques, if only in an informal way (Laurie, 1970). It is, however, a process which has yet to be formally developed, evaluated and introduced as an integral part of criminal investigation procedures. Research by the Stamford Research Institute and reported by Eck (1978) provides guidelines for the way in which research in this area might be developed.

ii. Specialist patrolling
Officers patrolling an area on foot or by car have in the past been deployed in the expectation that they will carry out a range of duties and control a variety

of crimes. Research has shown, however, that changes in the number of officers patrolling an area appear to be unrelated to the volume of crime reported. It may be that this is a consequence of relying on a form of policing which is too unfocussed, and that tactics designed to achieve limited but more precise objectives would be more successful. Such forms of policing offer the opportunity to identify the skills necessary to commit the crime, to recognise those criminals possessing such skills, and to study the particular locations within which the crime is likely to be committed. Given this information it is possible for the police to plan their activities in some detail, and direct their attention either to particular locations or particular offenders.

Despite the potential value of this form of patrolling few evaluations have been carried out. However, some evidence suggests that gains in crime control, where achieved by the deployment of specialist units, may well be offset by a deterioration in police/public relations. Undoubtedly the problem arises from the autonomy associated with, and necessary to, the formation of specialist units. Members of such units, by developing their own skills, by drawing on their sources of information, and by demonstrably achieving valued objectives, are in a strong position to resist supervision from senior officers. Under these circumstances the effectiveness of the police and the account-ability of the police to the public are in danger of standing in opposition to one another. It is important, therefore, that research in this area considers not only the effectiveness of the police but also their accountability to the community at large.

iii. Community policing
Community policing — an entirely different approach to police work — has yet to be fully evaluated. The attraction of community policing stems from the possibility it offers of drawing on public support for police work, and sharing with the public the responsibility for crime. Many activities falling under this heading rest on the assumption that crime is committed by those of a criminal mentality, and that it is an essential task of the police to inculcate in the public mind a sense of moral responsibility. Arguably, this process has some impact on the level of crime, but it is probably the case that many years must elapse before such effects become demonstrable. Situational policing — the form of community policing proposed by Engstad and Evans (1980) — by focussing, however, on particular crimes occurring at specific places, offers a better chance of significantly reducing crime within a relatively short period of time than other less well defined tactics.

The value of situational policing has yet to be empirically tested. But it will again be necessary to recognise that gains in effectiveness, where these are achieved by reorganising the relationship between the police and the public, may well raise issues regarding the accountability of the service. At the simplest level, where the police work for a greater degree of collaboration between themselves and local authority agencies, they are in danger of being criticised for stepping beyond their conventional role and for usurping the role of others; while on those occasions when the police urge the public to recognise, accept and act upon those aspects of crime to which they may be contributing, a position may arise in which the public find themselves accountable to the police.

The conclusions drawn from this review have fashioned the programme of research now proposed. In essence there is a need to identify those tasks the police can achieve and to develop appropriate tactics. Work of this nature can only be undertaken, if not by the police themselves, by research staff working in close collaboration with the police. Moreover it should be regarded as a contribution to a more general debate regarding the appropriate role of the police.

In summary, there are two particular points to be made regarding the programme itself. First, of the five tasks listed, it is probable that the identification of 'controllable crimes' should be seen as a primary focus for research effort. In carrying out this work much would undoubtedly be gained if it were to be complemented by research into the characteristics of crime and the psychological processes involved in committing and reporting criminal acts. Second, as to the tactics employed by the police, several authors have commented on the limited range of responses at the disposal of the police (Tien *et al.,* 1978). Thus, despite the diversity of crime and the complexity of the phenomenon, the police have traditionally been obliged to rely on the most general tactics. There is a need, therefore, to ensure that the diversity to be found between one crime and another is matched by an appropriate range of police tactics.

To date, the iconoclastic work of the researcher has led to the conclusion that the police have little effect on the level of crime. Some researchers have concluded that it is inappropriate even to use the concept of effectiveness in assessing police work (Hough, 1980). If correct, these conclusions have implications for the management of the police and for the content of future research programmes. However, it can be argued that most experimental studies have examined those aspects of policing which, with hindsight, had little chance of curtailing crime. Whatever the limitations of traditional policing tactics, the introduction of carefully designed strategies specifically tailored to tackle selected problems could still lead to control of some aspects of crime, and the achievement of crime related tasks. Research has a central part to play in the development and evaluation of such strategies.

References

Alderson, J. (1979). *Policing Freedom*. Plymouth, England: Macdonald and Evans.

Allison, J. P. (1972). 'Economic factors and the rate of crime'. *Land Economics,* 48, pp. 193 – 196.

Angell, J. A. (1971). 'Towards an alternative to the classic police organizational arrangements: a democratic model'. *Criminology,* 2, pp. 185 – 206.

Angell, J. E. (1975). *An Exploratory Study of Changes Accompanying The Implementation of a Community Based Participatory Team Policing Model*. Michigan State University, Michigan. (Unpublished).

Association of Chief Police Officers. (1979). *Report of a Working Party Appointed by the Association of Chief Police Officers on the Role of the Home Office Crime Prevention Centre, Stafford*. (Unpublished).

Ball, R. A. (1974). 'Quantitative evaluation of criminal justice programs'. In Viano, E. (Ed.), *Criminal Justice Research*. Lexington Mass: Lexington Books.

Banton, M. (1964). *The Policeman in the Community*. London: Tavistock.

Banton, M. (1974). 'Police'. *The New Encyclopedia Britannica: Macropaedia,* 14, pp. 662 – 671. London: Encyclopedia Britannica.

Banton, M. (1978). 'Crime prevention in the context of criminal policy'. *Police Studies,* 1, pp. 3 – 9.

Bayley, D. H. (1976). *Forces of Order: police behaviour in Japan and the United States*. Berkeley and Los Angeles: University of California Press.

Belson, W. A. (1978). *The Public and the Police*. London: Harper and Row.

Bercal, T. F. (1970). 'Calls for police assistance: consumer demands for government service'. In Hahn, H. (Ed.), *Police in Urban Society*. Beverley Hills, California: Sage Publications.

Berkley, G. E., Giles, M. W., Hackett, J. F. and Kassoff, N. C. (1976). *Introduction to Criminal Justice: police, courts, corrections*. Boston: Holbrook Press.

Biderman, A., Johnson, L., McIntyre, J. and Wier, A. (1967). *Report on a Pilot Study in the District of Colombia on Victimization and Attitudes Towards Law Enforcement. Field Study I.* Washington D.C.: US Government Printing Office.

Bieck, W. (1977). *Response Time Analysis.* Kansas City: Kansas City Police Department.

Bittner, E. (1970). *The Functions of the Police in Modern Society.* Chevy Chase, Md.: National Institute of Mental Health.

Bittner, E. (1974). 'Florence Nightingale in pursuit of Willie Sutton: a theory of the police'. In Jacob, H. (Ed.), *The Potential for Reform of Criminal Justice.* Beverly Hills, California: Sage Publications.

Blaber, A. (1979). *The Exeter Community Policing Consultative Group.* London: NACRO.

Block, P. and Weidman, D. (1975). *Managing Criminal Investigations.* Washington D.C.: United States Department of Justice.

Block, P. B. and Bell, J. (1976). *Managing Investigations: the Rochester System.* Washington D.C.: Police Foundation.

Bottomley, A. K. and Coleman, C. A. (1976). 'Criminal statistics: the police role in the discovery and detection of crime'. *International Journal of Criminology and Penology,* 4, pp. 33 – 58.

Bottomley, A. K. and Coleman, C. A. (1980). 'Understanding crime rates'. In Clarke, R. V. G. and Hough, J. M. (Eds.), *The Effectiveness of Policing.* Farnborough, England: Gower

Boydstun, J. (1975). *San Diego Field Interrogation.* Washington D.C.: Police Foundation.

Bright, J. A. (1969). *The Beat Patrol Experiment.* Home Office Police Research and Development Branch. (Unpublished).

Brown, D. W. (1978). 'Arrest rates and crime rates: when does a tipping effect occur?' *Social Forces,* 57, pp. 671 – 682.

Bunyard, R. S. (1978). *Police Organisation and Command.* Plymouth, England: McDonald and Evans.

Burrows, J. and Heal, K. H. (1979). 'Police car security campaigns'. In Burrows, J., Ekblom, P. and Heal, K. *Crime Prevention and the Police.* Home Office Research Study. No 55. London: HMSO.

Cain, M. (1971). 'On the beat'. In Cohen, S. (Ed.), *Images of Deviance.* London: Tavistock.

Cain, M. (1972). 'Police-professionalism: its meaning and consequences'. *Anglo-American Law Review,* 1, pp. 217 – 31.

Cain, M. (1973). *Society and the Policeman's Role*. London: Routledge and Kegan Paul.

Cain, M. (1977). 'An ironical departure: the dilemma of contemporary policing'. In Jones, K. (Ed.). *The Yearbook of Social Policy in Britain*. London: Routledge and Kegan Paul.

Cain, M. (1979). 'Trends in the sociology of police work'. *International Journal of Sociology of Law*, 7, pp. 143 – 167.

Carr-Hill, R. A. and Stern, N. H. (1979). *Crime: the police and criminal statistics*. London: Academic Press.

Chaiken, J. M., Lawless, M. W. and Stevenson, K. A. (1974). *The Impact of Police Activities on Crime: robberies in the New York City subway system*. Santa Monica, California: The Rand Corporation.

Chaiken, J. (1975). *The Criminal Investigation Process: survey of municipal and county police departments*. Santa Monica, California: Rand.

Chaiken, J. M. (1978). 'What is known about deterrent effects of police activities'. In Cramer, J. A. (Ed.), *Preventing Crime*. Beverley Hills, California: Sage Publications.

Chatterton, M. (1976). 'Police in social control'. In King, J. F. S. (Ed.), *Control Without Custody?* Cambridge: Institute of Criminology.

Chibnall, S. (1977). *Law and Order News*. London: Tavistock Publications.

Chibnall, S. (1979). 'The Metropolitan Police and the News Media'. In Holdaway, S. (Ed.), *The British Police*. London: Edward Arnold.

Clarke, R. V. G. (1980). 'Situational crime prevention: theory and practice'. *British Journal of Criminology*, 20, pp. 136 – 145.

Clarke, R. V. G. and Hough, J. M. (Eds.). (1980). *The Effectiveness of Policing*. Farnborough, England: Gower.

Clarke, R. V. G. and Mayhew, P. (Eds.). (1980). *Designing Out Crime*. London: HMSO.

Clawson, C. and Chang, S. (1977). 'The relationship of response delays and arrest rates'. *Institute of Police Science and Administration*, 5, pp. 53 – 68.

Coleman, C. A. and Bottomley, A. K. (1976). 'Police conceptions of crime and "no crime"'. *Criminal Law Review*, pp. 344 – 360.

Comrie, M. D. and Kings, E. J. (1975). *Study of Urban Workloads: final report*. Home Office Police Research Services Unit. (Unpublished).

Courtis, M. and Bussuyer, J. (1970). *Attitudes to Crime and the Police in Toronto. A Report of some Survey Findings*. Toronto: Centre of Criminology, University of Toronto.

Cox, B., Shirley, J. and Short, M. (1977). *The Fall of Scotland Yard.* Harmondsworth: Penguin Books.

Croft, J. (1979). *Crime and the Community.* Home Office Research Study No. 50. London: HMSO.

Crust, P. E. (1975). *Criminal Investigation Project.* Home Office Police Research Services Unit. (Unpublished).

Cumberbatch, G. and Beardsworth, A. (1976). 'Criminals, victims and mass communications'. In Viano, E. (Ed.), *Victims and Society.* Washington: Visage Press.

Eck, J. E. (1978). *Burglary Investigation Decision Model Replication: a multisite evaluation.* Paper presented to LEAA. National Workshop of Criminal Evaluation (Unpublished).

Edgar, J. M., Marcus, M. M., Wheaton, R. J. and Hicox, R. C. (1976). *Team Policing.* Washington, D.C.: LEAA.

Ekblom, P. (1979). 'Police truancy patrols'. In Burrows, J., Ekblom, P. and Heal, K. *Crime Prevention and the Police.* Home Office Research Study No. 55. London: HMSO.

Elliott, J. F. (1973). *Interception Patrol.* Springfield, Illinois: Charles Thomas.

Elliott, J. F. (1978). 'Crime control teams: an alternative of the conventional operational procedure of investigatory crimes'. *Institute of Criminal Justices,* 6, pp. 11 – 23.

Engstad, P. and Lioy, M. (Eds.). (1979). *Proceedings: workshop on police productivity and performance.* Ottawa, Ont.: Solicitor General of Canada.

Engstad, P. and Evans, A. (1980). 'Responsibility, competence and police effectiveness in crime control'. In Clarke, R. V. G. and Hough, J. M. (Eds.), *The Effectiveness of Policing.* Farnborough, England: Gower.

Ericson, R. V. (1978). *Reproducing Order: a study of police patrol work.* Toronto: Centre of Criminology, University of Toronto. (Unpublished).

Ericson, R. V. (1978). *Making Crime: a study of detective work.* Toronto: Centre of Criminology, University of Toronto. (Unpublished).

Farmer, D. J. (1980). 'Out of the hugger-mugger: the case of police field services'. In Clarke, R. V. G. and Hough, J. M. (Eds.), *The Effectiveness of Policing.* Farnborough, England: Gower.

Fienberg, S., Kinley, L. and Reiss, A. J. (1976). 'Redesigning the Kansas City preventive-patrol experiment'. *Evaluation,* 3, pp. 124 – 131.

Fisk, D. (1970). *The Indianapolis Police Fleet Plan.* Washington D.C.: Urban Institute.

Fisk, J. (1974). *The Police Officer's Exercise of Discretion in the Decision to Arrest: relationship and organisational goals and societal values.* Los Angeles: University College, Institute of Government and Public Affairs.

Forst, B., Lucianoric, J. and Cox, S. J. (1977). *What Happens After Arrest?* Washington D.C.: Institute of Law and Social Research.

Gelles, R. J. (1972). *The Violent Home: a study of physical aggression between husband and wives.* London: Sage Publications.

Gelles, R. J. (1976). 'Abused wives: why do they stay?'. *Journal of Marriage and the Family,* 38, pp. 659 – 668.

Goldstein, H. (1975). *Police Corruption: a perspective on its nature and control.* Washington D.C.: Police Foundation.

Goldstein, H. (1977). *Policing a Free Society.* Cambridge, Mass. Ballinger.

Goldstein, H. (1979). 'Improving policing: a problem-oriented approach'. *Crime and Delinquency,* 25, pp. 236 – 258.

Government Social Survey Central Office of Information. (1962). *The Relations Between the Police and the Public—appendix 4 to the Minutes of Evidence: Royal Commission on Police 1962.* London: HMSO.

Greenwood, M. and Wadycki, W. (1973). 'Crime rates and public expenditure for police protection: their interaction'. *Review of Social Economy,* 31, pp. 138 – 151.

Greenwood, P. W., Chaiken, J. M., Petersila, J. and Prusoff, L. (1977). *The Criminal Investigation Process.* Lexington, Mass: D. C. Heath.

Hall, S., Critcher, C., Jefferson, T., Clarke, J. and Roberts, B. (1978). *Policing the Crisis: mugging, the state, and law and order.* London: MacMillan.

Haller, M. H. (1976). 'Historical roots of police behaviour: Chicago 1890 – 1925'. *Law and Society Review,* 10, pp. 303 – 323.

Halper, A. and Ku, R. (1975). *New York City Police Department Street Crime Unit: an exemplary project.* Washington D.C.: Law Enforcement Assistance Administration.

Harris, L. and Associates. (1972). American Institute of Public Opinion. Study No. 861.

Hatry, H. P. (1975). 'Wrestling with police crime control productivity measurement'. In Wolfe, J. F. and Heaphy, J. L. (Eds.), *Readings on Productivity in Policing.* Washington D.C.: Police Foundation.

Heller, N. B. (1977). *A Review of Police Research in the United States.* The Institute of Public Program Analysis, St Louis, USA. (Unpublished).

Heywood, R. (1979). 'Traditional and innovative policing'. In Engstad, P. and Lioy, M. (Eds.). *Proceedings: workshop on police productivity and performance.* Ottawa, Ont.: Solicitor General's Office.

Hindelang, M. J., Dunn, C. S., Aumick, A. L. and Sutton, L. P. (1975). *Sourcebook of Criminal Justice Statistics.* Washington D.C.: Government Printing Office.

Hindelang, M. J. (1976). *Criminal Victimization in Eight American Cities.* Cambridge, Mass.: Ballinger.

Hirsch, G. and Riccio, L. (1974). 'Measuring and improving the productivity of police patrols'. *Journal of Police Science and Administration,* 2, pp. 169 – 184.

Holdaway, S. (1977). 'Changes in urban policing'. *British Journal of Sociology,* 28, pp. 119 – 137.

Holdaway, S. (1979). *The British Police.* London: Edward Arnold.

Hough, J. M. (1980). 'Managing with less technology: the impact of information technology on police management'. *British Journal of Criminology,* 20, pp. 344 – 357.

Hough, J. M. and Heal, K. H. (1979). 'Police effectiveness: some popular misconceptions'. *Home Office Research Bulletin,* 7, pp. 16 – 19. London: Home Office Research Unit.

Hough, J. M. (1980). *Uniformed Police Work and Management Technology.* Research Unit Paper 1. London: Home Office.

Ignatieff, M. (1979). 'Police and people: the birth of Mr Peel's blue locusts'. *New Society,* pp. 443 – 445.

Isaacs, H. H. (1967). 'A study of communications, crimes and arrests in the Metropolitan Police Department'. *Task Force Report: science and technology.* Washington D.S.: US. Government Printing Office.

James, D. (1979). 'Police-black relations: the professional solution'. In Holdaway, S. (Ed.), *The British Police.* London: Edward Arnold.

Jefferson, T. (1979). 'Review article'. *British Journal of Criminology,* 1, pp. 76 – 79.

Junger—Tas, J. (1978). *The Dutch and Their Police.* The Hague: Research and Documentation Centre of the Ministry of Justice. (Unpublished).

Kelling, G., Pate, T., Diekmand, D. and Brown, C. (1974). *The Kansas City Preventive Patrol Experiment.* Washington, D.C.: Police Foundation.

Kelling, G. (1977). *A Proposal to Evaluate the Effects of Foot Patrol.* Washington D.C.: Police Foundation. (Unpublished).

Kelling, G. (1978). 'Police field service and crime: the presumed effects of a capacity'. *Crime and Delinquency,* 24, pp. 178 – 184.

Kelling, G., Wycoff, M. A. and Pate, T. (1980). 'Policing: a research agenda for rational policy making'. In Clarke, R. V. G. and Hough, J. M. (Eds.), *The Effectiveness of Policing.* Farnborough, England: Gower.

Kelling, G. and Pate, T. (1980). *The New Jersey Foot Patrol Experiment: executive summary.* Washington, D.C.: Police Foundation (Unpublished).

Knights, Sir P. (1980). *Preventive Policing: inner city perspective.* Paper presented at the 1980 Cranfield Conference. Bedford, England: Cranfield Institute of Technology. (Unpublished).

Lambert, J. R. (1970). *Crime, Police and Race Relations.* London: Oxford University Press.

Larson, R. C. (1972). *Urban Police Patrol Analysis.* Cambridge, Mass.: MIT Press.

Larson, R. C. (1976). 'What happened to patrol operations in Kansas City? A review of the Kansas City preventive patrol experiment'. *Journal of Criminal Justice,* 3, pp. 267 – 297.

Laugharne, A. (1980). *Skelmersdale Co-ordinated Policing Experiment.* Paper presented at the Cranfield Conference. Bedford, England: Cranfield Institute of Technology. (Unpublished).

Laurie, P. (1970). *Scotland Yard: a personal enquiry.* London: Bodley Head.

Levi-Strauss, C. (1966). *The Savage Mind.* London: Weidenfeld and Nicolson.

Ley, D. and Cybriniwsky, R. (1974). 'The spatial ecology of stripped cars' *Environment and Behaviour,* 6, pp. 53 – 67.

Logan, C. H. (1975). 'Arrest rates and deterrence'. *Social Science Quarterly,* 55, pp. 376 – 389.

McBarnet, D. J. (1979). 'Arrest: the legal context of policing'. In Holdaway, S. (Ed.), *The British Police.* London: Edward Arnold.

McCabe, S. and Sutcliffe, F. (1978). *Defining Crime: a study of police decisions.* Oxford: Blackwell.

McDowell, C. (1971). 'The police as victims of their own misconceptions'. *Journal of Criminal Law, Criminology and Police Science,* 62, pp. 430 – 436.

Manning, P. (1977). *Police Work: the special organisation of policing.* London: MIT Press.

Manolias, M. (1980). *The Gainsborough Experiment in Community Policing.* Home Office Police Scientific Development Branch. (Unpublished).

Mark, Sir R. (1971). *Speech given to the Institute of Journalists on 30 November 1971*. London: New Scotland Yard. (Unpublished).

Martin, J. and Wilson, G. (1969). *The Police: a study in manpower*. London: Heinemann.

Matza, D. (1969). *Becoming Deviant*. Englewood Cliffs, New Jersey: Prentice Hall.

Mawby, R. (1979). *Policing the City*. Farnborough, England: Saxon House.

Mayhew, P., Clarke, R. V. G., Hough, J. M. and Sturman, A. (1976). *Crime as Opportunity*. Home Office Research Study No. 34. London: HMSO.

Mayhew, P., Clarke, R. V. G., Burrows, J. N., Hough, J. M. and Winchester, S. W. C. (1979). *Crime in Public View*. Home Office Research Study No. 49. London: HMSO.

Miller, W. (1977a). 'Never on Sunday: moralistic reformers and the police in London and New York City 1830 – 1870'. In Bayley, D. H. (Ed.), *Police and Society*. London: Sage Publications.

Miller, W. (1977b). *Cops and Bobbies: police authority in New York and London 1830 – 1870*. Chicago: University of Chicago Press.

Morris, N. and Hawkins, G. (1977). *Letter to the President on Crime Control*. Chicago: University of Chicago Press.

New York Police Department. (1955). *Operation 25*.

Nichols, J. F. and Bannon, J. D. (1972). 'S.T.R.E.S.S. zero visibility policing'. *Police Chief*. Vol. 39, pp. 33 – 36

Nilsson, E. (1980). *Current Research Projects at the National Swedish Police Board*. Paper presented at a meeting of the Home Office Research Unit, London. (Unpublished).

O'Malley, H. C. (1973). *Evaluation Report on the Holyoke Team Policing Experiment*. Massachusetts: Holyoke Police Department. (Unpublished).

Parkinson, G. (1977). *Figuring It Out*. Victoria, B.C.: British Columbia Justice Development Commission.

Parnas, R. I. (1971). 'Police discretion and the diversion of incidents of intra-family violence. *Law and Contempary Problems*, 36, pp. 539 – 565.

Pate, T, Ferrara, A., Bowers, R. and Lorence, J. (1976). *Police Response Time: its determinants and effects*. Washington D.C.: Police Foundation.

Pate, T. Bowers, B. A. and Parks, R. (1976). *Three Approaches to Criminal Apprehension in Kansas City. An Evaluation Report*. Washington D.C.: Police Foundation.

Perrier, D. (1979). 'Is policing a profession?'. *Canadian Journal of Criminology*, 21, pp. 52 – 70.

Phillips, L. and Votey, H. L. (1972). 'An economic analysis of the deterrent effects of law enforcement on criminal activity'. *Journal of Criminal Law, Criminology and Police Science*, 63, pp. 330 – 342.

Pollard, B. (1979). 'Evaluating a preventive project'. In Brown, J. and Howes, G. (Eds.), *The Cranfield Papers. The Proceedings of the 1978 Cranfield Conference on the Prevention of Crime in Europe*. London: Peel Press.

Pollard, B. (1979). *A Study of the Leicestershire Constabulary Highfields Community Policing Scheme*. Bedford, England: Cranfield Institute of Technology. (Unpublished).

President's Commission on Law Enforcement and Administration of Justice. (1967). *Task Force Report: the police*. Washington, D.C.: Government Printing Office.

Press, J. S. (1971). *Some Effects of an Increase in Police Manpower in the 20th Precinct of New York City*. New York: Rand Institute.

Pressman, I. and Carol A. (1971). 'Crime as a diseconomy of scale'. *Review of Social Economy*, 29, pp. 227 – 236.

Pullé, S. (1973). *Police-Immigrant Relations in Ealing*. London: Runnymede Trust.

Punch, M. and Naylor, T. (1973). 'The police: a social service'. *New Society*, 24, pp. 358 – 361.

Punch, M. (1979). *Policing the Inner City*. London: MacMillan Press.

Reinar, R. (1978). *The Blue-Coated Worker: a sociological study of police unionism*. Cambridge: Cambridge University Press.

Reiss, A. J. and Bordua, D. J. (1967). 'Environment and organization: a perspective on the police'. In Bordua, D. J. (Ed), *The Police: six sociological essays*. New York: Wiley.

Reiss, A. J. (1971). *The Police and the Public*. New Haven: Yale University Press.

Riccio, L. J. (1978). 'Police data as a guide for measuring productivity' In Cohen, S. (Ed.), *The Future of Policing*. Beverley Hills, California: Sage Publications.

Sanders, W. (1977). *Detective Work: a study of criminal investigations*. New York: Free Press.

Schaffer, E. B. (1980). *Community Policing*. London: Croom Helm.

Schnelle, J. F., Kirchner, R. E., McNees, M. P., and Lawler, J. M. (1975). 'Social evaluation research: the evaluation of two police patrolling strategies'. *Journal of Applied Behaviour Analysis*, 4, pp. 353 – 365.

Schnelle, J. F., Kirchner, R. E., Casey, J. D., Uselton, P. H. and McNees, M. P. (1977). 'Patrol evaluation research: a multiple-baseline analysis of saturation police patrolling during day and night hours'. *Journal of Applied Behaviour Analysis*, 10, pp. 33 – 40.

Schwartz, A. I. and Sumner, N. C. (1974). *The Cincinnati Team Policing Experiment*. Washington D.C.: Police Foundation.

Shaw, M. and Williamson, W. (1972). 'Public attitudes to the police'. *Criminologist*, 7, pp. 18 – 33.

Sherman, L. W., Milton, C. H. and Kelly, T. V. (1973). *Team Policing: seven case studies*. Washington D.C.: Police Foundation.

Silver, A. (1967). 'The demand for order in civil society: a review of some themes in the history of urban crime, police and riot'. In Bordua, D. (Ed), *The Police: six sociological essays*. New York: Wiley.

Sjoquist, D. L. (1973). 'Property crime and economic behaviour; some empirical results'. *American Economic Review*, 63, pp. 439 – 446.

Skogan, W. G. (Ed.), (1976). *Sample Surveys of the Victims of Crime*. Cambridge, Mass: Ballinger Publishing Company.

Skolnick, J. (1966). *Justice Without Trial*. New York: Wiley.

Smith, P. and Hawkins, R. (1973). 'Victimization types of citizen-police contacts and attitudes toward the police'. *Law and Society*, 8, pp. 135 – 152.

Softley, P., Brown, D., Forde, B., Mair, G. and Moxon, D. (1980). *Police Interrogation*. Home Office Research Study No. 61. London: HMSO.

Sparks, R. F., Genn, H. G., and Dodd, D. J. (1977). *Surveying Victims*. London: Wiley.

Steer, D. (1980). *Uncovering Crime: the role of the police*. Royal Commission on Criminal Procedure. Research Study No. 7. London: HMSO.

Stinchcombe, A. (1963). 'Institutions of privacy in the determination of police administrative practice'. *American Journal of Sociology*, 69, pp. 150 – 160.

Sussex Police. (1976). *Development of the Criminal Investigation Element of Force and Special Inquiry Units*. Organisational and Planning Department. (Unpublished).

Sweeney, T. J. and Illingsworth, W. (Eds.). (1973). *Issues in Police Patrol*. Washington D.C.: Police Foundation.

Thomas, C. and Hyman, J. (1977). 'Perception of crime fear of victimization and public perception of police performance'. *Journal of Police Science and Administration*, 5, pp. 305 – 317.

Tien, J., Simon, J. and Larson, R. (1978). *An Alternative Approach in Police Patrols: the Wilmington split force experiment*. Cambridge, Mass: Public Systems Evaluation.

Tittle, C. R. and Rowe, A. (1974). 'Certainty of arrest and crime rates. A further test of the deterrent hypothesis'. *Social Forces*, 52, pp. 455 – 462.

Treger, H. (1980). *Problems and Issues in Police/Social Work Co-operation*. Paper presented at 1980 the Cranfield Conference. Bedford, England: Cranfield Institute of Technology. (Unpublished).

Tullock, G. (1965). *The Politics of Bureaucracy*. Washington D.C.: Public Affairs Press.

Walsh, J. L. (1977). 'Career styles and police behaviour'. In Bayley, D. (Ed.), *Police and Society*. London: Sage Publications.

Wasson, D. K. (1975). *Community-Based Preventive Policing: a review*. Ottowa, Ont.: Solicitor General Canada.

Werthman, C. and Piliavin, I. (1967). 'Gang members and the police'. In Bordua, D. J. (Ed.), *The Police: six sociological essays*. London: Wiley.

Westinghouse National Issues Centre. (1979). *What Happened: an examination of recently terminated anti-fencing operations*. Washington D.C.: Law Enforcement Assistance Administration.

Westley, W. A. (1970). *Violence and the Police: a sociological study of law, custom and morality*. Cambridge, Mass.: MIT PRESS.

Whitaker, B. (1964). *The Police*. Harmondsworth: Penguin Books.

Whitaker, B. (1979). *The Police in Society*. London: Eyre Methuen.

Whyte, W. F. (1955). *Street Corner Society*. Chicago: University of Chicago Press.

Wilson, J. Q. (1968). *Varieties of Police Behaviour*. Cambridge, Mass.: Harvard University Press.

Wilson, J. Q. (1975). *Thinking About Crime*. New York: Basic Books.

Wilson, J. Q. and Boland, B. (1976). 'Crime'. In Gorham, W and Glazer, N. (Eds.), *The Urban Predicament*. Washington D.C.: The Urban Institute.

Wilson, J. Q. and Boland, B. (1978). 'The effect of the police on crime'. *Law and Society Review*, 12, pp. 367 – 390.

Wilson, O. W. and McLaren, R. C. (1963). *Police Administration*. New York: McGraw-Hill.

Woodley, A. C. (1976). *Thames Valley Collator Project*. Home Office Police Scientific Development Branch. (Unpublished).

Zander, M. (1974). 'Aquittal rates and not guilty pleas: what do the statistics mean?'. *Criminal Law Review*. pp. 401 – 408.

Publications

5. †Financial penalties and probation. Martin Davies. 1970. vii + 38pp. (11 340105 1) 30p.

6. Hostels for probationers. Study of the aims, working and variations in the effectiveness of male probation hostels with special reference to the influence of the environment on delinquency. Ian Sinclair. 1971. iv + 199pp. (11 340106 X) £1.15.

7. Prediction methods in criminology including a prediction study of young men on probation. Frances H. Simon. 1971. xi + 233pp. (11 340107 8) £1.25.

8. †Study of the juvenile liaison scheme in West Ham 1961 – 1965. Marilyn Taylor. 1971. vi + 45pp. (11 340108 6) 35p.

9. †Explorations in after-care. I—After-care units in London, Liverpool and Manchester. Martin Silberman (Royal London Prisoners' Aid Society), Brenda Chapman. II—After-care hostels receiving a Home Office grant. Ian Sinclair and David Snow (HORU). III—St Martin of Tours House. Aryeh Leissner (National Bureau for Co-operation in Child Care). 1971. xi + 168pp. (11 340109 4) 85p.

10. A survey of adoption in Great Britain. Eleanor Grey in collaboration with R. M. Blunden. 1971. ix + 168pp. (11 340110 8) 95p.

11. †Thirteen-year-old approved school boys in 1962. Elizabeth Field, W. H. Hammond and J. Tizard. 1971. ix + 45pp. (11 340111 6) 35p.

12. Absconding from approved schools. R. V. G. Clarke and D. N. Martin. 1971. vi + 145pp. (11 340112 4) 85p.

13. An experiment in personality assessment of young men remanded in custody. H. Sylvia Anthony. 1972. viii + 79pp. (11 340113 2) 52½p.

14. Girl offenders aged 17 – 20 years. I—Statistics relating to girl offenders aged 17 – 20 years from 1960 to 1970. II—Re-offending by girls released from borstal or detention centre training. III—The problems of girls released from borstal training during their period on after-care. Jean Davies and Nancy Goodman. 1972. v + 77pp. (11 340114 0) 52½p.

15. †The controlled trial in institutional research—paradigm or pitfall for penal evaluators? R. V. G. Clarke and D. B. Cornish. 1972. v + 33pp. (11 340115 9) 29p.

16. A survey of fine enforcement. Paul Softley. 1973. v + 65pp. (11 340116 7) 47p.

17. †An index of social environment designed for use in social work research. Martin Davies. 1973. v + 61pp. (11 340117 5) 47p.

18. †Social enquiry reports and the probation service. Martin Davies and Andrea Knopf. 1973. v + 47pp. (11 340118 3) 50p.

19. †Depression, psychopathic personality and attempted suicide in a borstal sample. H. Sylvia Anthony. 1973. viii + 44pp. (0 11 340119 1) 36½p.

20. The use of bail and custody by London magistrates' courts before and after the Criminal Justice Act 1967. Frances Simon and Mollie Weatheritt. 1974. vi + 78pp. (0 11 340120 5) 57p.

21. Social work in the environment. A study of one aspect of probation practice. Martin Davies, with Margaret Rayfield, Alaster Calder and Tony Fowles. 1974. x + 164pp. (0 11 340121 3) £1.10.

22. Social work in prisons. An experiment in the use of extended contact with offenders. Margaret Shaw. 1974. viii + 156pp. (0 11 340122 1) £1.45.

23. Delinquency amongst opiate users. Joy Mott and Marilyn Taylor. 1974. vi + 54pp. (0 11 340663 0) 41p.

24. IMPACT. Intensive matched probation and after-care treatment. Vol. 1. The design of the probation experiment and an interim evaluation. M. S. Folkard, A. J. Fowles, B. C. McWilliams, W. McWilliams, D. D. Smith, D. E. Smith and G. R. Walmsley. 1974. vi + 54pp. (0 11 340664 9) £1.25.

25. The approved school experience. An account of boys' experience of training under differing regimes of approved schools, with an attempt to evaluate the effectiveness of that training. Anne B. Dunlop. 1974. viii + 124pp. (0 11 340665 7). £1.22.

†Out of print. Photostat copies can be purchased from Her Majesty's Stationery Office upon request.

26. Absconding from open prisons. Charlotte Banks, Patricia Mayhew and R. J. Sapsford. 1975. viii + 92pp. (0 11 340666 5) 95p.

27. Driving while disqualified. Sue Kriefman. 1975. vi + 138pp. (0 11 340667 3) £1.22.

28. Some male offenders' problems. I—Homeless offenders in Liverpool. W. McWilliams. II—Casework with short-term prisoners. Julie Holborn. 1975. x + 150pp. (0 11 340668 1) £2.50.

29. Community service orders. K. Pease, P. Durkin, I. Earnshaw, D. Payne and J. Thorpe. 1975. viii + 80pp. (0 11 340669 X) 75p.

30. Field Wing Bail Hostel: the first nine months. Frances Simon and Sheena Wilson. 1975. viii + 56pp. (0 11 340670 3) 85p.

31. Homicide in England and Wales 1967 – 1971. Evelyn Gibson. 1975. iv + 60pp. (0 11 340753 X) 90p.

32. Residential treatment and its effects on delinquency. D. B. Cornish and R. V. G. Clarke. 1975. vi + 74pp. (0 11 340672 X) £1.00.

33. Further studies of female offenders. Part A: Borstal girls eight years after release. Nancy Goodman, Elizabeth Maloney and Jean Davies. Part B: The sentencing of women at the London Higher Courts. Nancy Goodman, Paul Durkin and Janet Halton. Part C: Girls appearing before a juvenile court. Jean Davies. 1976. vi + 114pp. (0 11 340673 8) £1.55.

34. Crime as opportunity. P. Mayhew, R. V. G. Clarke, A. Sturman and J. M. Hough. 1976. vii + 36pp. (0 11 340674 6) 70p.

35. The effectiveness of sentencing: a review of the literature. S. R. Brody. 1976. v + 89pp. (0 11 340675 4) £1.15.

36. IMPACT. Intensive matched probation and after-care treatment. Vol. II—The results of the experiment. M. S. Folkard, D. E. Smith and D. D. Smith. 1976. xi + 40pp. (0 11 340676 2) 80p.

37. Police cautioning in England and Wales. J. A. Ditchfield. 1976. iv + 31pp. (0 11 340677 0) 65p.

38. Parole in England and Wales. C. P. Nuttall, with E. E. Barnard, A. J. Fowles, A. Frost, W. H. Hammond, P. Mayhew, K. Pease, R. Tarling and M. J. Weatheritt. 1977. vi + 90pp. (0 11 340678 9) £1.75.

39. Community service assessed in 1976. K. Pease, S. Billingham and I. Earnshaw. 1977. vi + 29pp. (0 11 340679 7) 75p.

40. Screen violence and film censorship. Stephen Brody. 1977. vi + 179pp. (0 11 340680 0) £2.75.

41. Absconding from borstals. Gloria K. Laycock. 1977. v + 82pp. (0 11 340681 9) £1.50.

42. Gambling—a review of the literature and its implications for policy and research. D. B. Cornish. 1978. xii + 284pp. (0 11 340682 7) £4.25.

43. Compensation orders in magistrates' courts. Paul Softley. 1978. vi + 41pp. (0 11 340683 5) 90p.

44. Research in criminal justice. John Croft. 1978. vi + 16pp. (0 11 340684 3) 50p.

45. Prison welfare: an account of an experiment at Liverpool. A. J. Fowles. 1978. v + 34pp. (0 11 340685 1) 75p.

46. Fines in magistrates' courts. Paul Softley. 1978. v + 42pp. (0 11 340686 X) £1.00.

47. Tackling vandalism. R. V. G. Clarke (editor), F. J. Gladstone, A. Sturman and Sheena Wilson (contributors). 1978. vi + 91pp. (0 11 340687 8) £4.00.

48. Social inquiry reports: a survey. Jennifer Thorpe. 1979. vi + 55pp. (0 11 340688 6) £1.50.

49. Crime in public view. P. Mayhew, R. V. G. Clarke, J. N. Burrows, J. M. Hough and S. W. C. Winchester. 1979. v + 36pp. (0 11 340689 4) £1.00.

50. Crime and the community. John Croft. 1979. v + 16pp. (0 11 340690 8) 65p.

51. Life-sentence prisoners. David Smith (editor), Christopher Brown, Joan Worth, Roger Sapsford and Charlotte Banks (contributors). 1979. v + 52pp. (0 11 340691 6) £1.25.

52. Hostels for offenders. Jane E. Andrews with an appendix by Bill Sheppard. 1979. v + 30pp. (0 11 340692 4) £1.50.

53. Previous convictions, sentence and reconviction: a statistical study of a sample of 5,000 offenders convicted in January 1971. G. J. O. Phillpotts and L. B. Lancucki. 1979. v + 55pp. (0 11 340693 2) £2.25.

54. Sexual offences, consent and sentencing. Roy Walmsley and Karen White. 1979. vi + 77pp. (0 11 340694 0) £2.75.

55. Crime prevention and the police. John Burrows, Paul Ekblom and Kevin Heal. 1979. v + 37pp. (0 11 340695 9) £1.75.

56. Sentencing practice in magistrates' courts. Roger Tarling with the assistance of Mollie Weatheritt. 1979. vii + 54pp. (0 11 340696 7) £2.25.

57. Crime and comparative research. John Croft. 1979. iv + 16pp. (0 11 340697 5). £1.00

58. Race, crime and arrests. Philip Stevens and Carole F. Willis. 1979. v + 69pp. (0 11 340698 3) £2.75.

59. Research and criminal policy. John Croft. 1980. iv + 14pp. (0 11 340699 1) £1.75.

60. Junior attendance centres. Anne B. Dunlop. 1980. v + 47pp. (0 11 340700 9) £2.75.

61. Police interrogation: an observational study in four police stations. Paul Softley with the assistance of David Brown, Bob Forde, George Mair and David Moxon. 1980. vii + 67pp. (0 11 340701 7). £3.90.

62. Co-ordinating crime prevention efforts. F. J. Gladstone. 1980. v + 74pp. (0 11 340702 5). £3.90.

63. Crime prevention publicity: an assessment. D. Riley and P. Mayhew. 1980. v + 47pp. (0 11 340703 3). £3.30.

64. Taking offenders out of circulation. Stephen Brody and Roger Tarling. 1980. v + 46pp. (0 11 340704 1) £3.00.

65. Alcoholism and social policy: are we on the right lines? Mary Tuck. 1980. v + 30pp. (0 11 340705 X) £2.70.

66. Persistent petty offenders. Suzan Fairhead. 1981. vi + 78 pp. (0 11 340706 8). £3.90.

HMSO

The above publications can be purchased from the Government Bookshops at the addresses listed on cover page iv (post orders to PO Box 569, London SE1 9NH) or through booksellers.

The following Home Office research publications are available on request from the Home Office Research Unit. Information Section, 50 Queen Anne's Gate, London, SW1H 9AT.

Research Unit Papers

1. Uniformed police work and management technology. J. M. Hough. 1980.

2. Supplementary information on sexual offences and sentencing. Roy Walmsley and Karen White. 1980.

Research Bulletin

The Research Bulletin is normally published twice a year and consists mainly of short articles relating to projects which are part of the Home Office Research Unit's research programme.

Printed in England for Her Majesty's Stationery Office by Hobbs the Printers of Southampton
(624) Dd0716575 C17 6/81 G327